T0316511

Cambridge Elements ☰

Elements in Eighteenth-Century Connections
edited by
Eve Tavor Bannet
University of Oklahoma
Rebecca Bullard
University of Reading

VOLTAIRE'S CORRESPONDENCE

Digital Readings

Nicholas Cronk
University of Oxford
Glenn Roe
Sorbonne University
Co-Directors of the Voltaire Lab,
Voltaire Foundation, University of Oxford

CAMBRIDGE
UNIVERSITY PRESS

CAMBRIDGE
UNIVERSITY PRESS

University Printing House, Cambridge CB2 8BS, United Kingdom

One Liberty Plaza, 20th Floor, New York, NY 10006, USA

477 Williamstown Road, Port Melbourne, VIC 3207, Australia

314–321, 3rd Floor, Plot 3, Splendor Forum, Jasola District Centre,
New Delhi – 110025, India

79 Anson Road, #06–04/06, Singapore 079906

Cambridge University Press is part of the University of Cambridge.

It furthers the University's mission by disseminating knowledge in the pursuit of
education, learning, and research at the highest international levels of excellence.

www.cambridge.org
Information on this title: www.cambridge.org/9781108791724
DOI: 10.1017/9781108866552

© Nicholas Cronk and Glenn Roe 2020

First published 2020

A catalogue record for this publication is available from the British Library.

ISBN 978-1-108-79172-4 Paperback
ISSN 2632-5578 (online)
ISSN 2632-556X (print)

Voltaire's Correspondence

Digital Readings

Elements in Eighteenth-Century Connections

DOI: 10.1017/9781108866552
First published online: November 2020

Nicholas Cronk
University of Oxford

Glenn Roe
Sorbonne University

Author for correspondence: Glenn Roe, glenn.roe@sorbonne-universite.fr

Abstract: Voltaire's correspondence has been described as his greatest masterpiece – but if it is, it is also his least studied. One of the most prodigious correspondences in Western literature, it poses significant interpretative challenges to the critic and reader alike. Considered individually, the letters present a series of complex, subtle, and playful literary performances; taken together, they constitute a formidable, and even forbidding, ensemble. How can modern readers even attempt to understand such an imposing work? This Element addresses this question through the use of digital reading methods and resources that enhance our understanding of this complex literary object and its relationship to Voltaire's more canonical literary output, and indeed to the Enlightenment world at large. Our aim is to provide scholars and students with new pathways into this particular corpus, using tools and approaches that can then be applied to correspondences and life-writing texts in all languages and periods.

Keywords: Voltaire, correspondence, digital humanities, distant reading, Enlightenment

ISBNs: 9781108791724 (PB), 9781108866552 (OC)
ISSNs: 2632-5578 (online), 2632-556X (print)

Contents

1 Beginnings

1.1 Introduction

Voltaire's correspondence stands as one of the great literary monuments of the eighteenth century. The corpus of over 21,000 letters, of which more than 15,000 are by Voltaire himself, addressing some 1,800 correspondents, is impressive – and somewhat overwhelming (see Mervaud, 2009). Historians and literary critics who use this correspondence frequently employ it instrumentally to establish a date or confirm a fact, and only rarely have critics attempted to examine this epistolary corpus in its entirety and to understand it as a literary whole. Its sheer size is clearly part of the problem, making it an ideal test case for examining the pros and cons of 'close' and 'distant' reading. The aim of this essay is to experiment with a range of digital humanities methods and to explore to what extent they can help us to identify new interpretative approaches to what is possibly Voltaire's greatest masterpiece.

1.2 Voltaire's Correspondence as Literary Object

Letters versus Correspondence

If the correspondence is Voltaire's masterpiece, it is not one that he consciously set out to write.[1] It may therefore be helpful to begin by describing how the epistolary corpus that we have today came into being. A distinction needs to be made between 'letters' and 'correspondence': the survival of individual letters may be a matter of serendipity, whereas a correspondence depends on systematic exchanges – on a network, in fact – and a network can only thrive in particular social and economic circumstances. Improved roads meant that postal services became markedly more regular and reliable in the eighteenth century, and the reliability of the postal service in turn nurtured the growth of Enlightenment correspondence networks – as in this depiction of the postal network in France (see Fig. 1.1).

Voltaire spent most of his adult life away from the French capital, and letters played a vital role in sustaining his career, keeping him abreast of the news, helping him nurture relationships old and new and in general remain a dynamic presence in the literary world of Paris. If Diderot's correspondence, remarkable in its quality, seems disappointingly small, that is because, unlike Voltaire, he saw his friends in Paris regularly and did not need to write to them to stay in touch. Increasingly, letters became for Voltaire a literary form of choice: he wrote essays and articles in the style of letters and used 'real' letters in his

---

[1] The argument of the following paragraphs is expanded in Cronk, 2019.

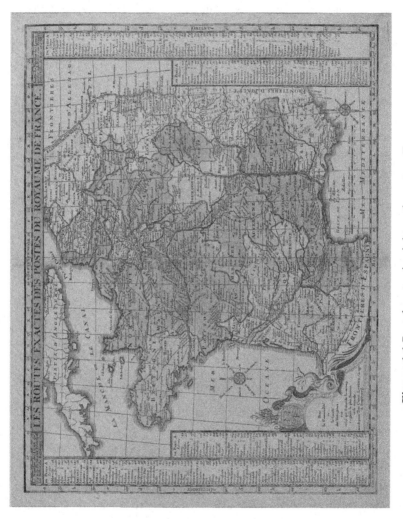

Figure 1.1 Postal routes in eighteenth-century France

imaginative works as well as imaginary letters in his non-fiction works – his predilection for manipulating the letter form is something of an obsession, an aspect of his writing that remains insufficiently explored.

Some authors self-consciously construct their correspondence as a literary object by recording their complete epistolary corpus: George Washington, clearly sensitive to his place in history, employed a copy press (a device that made copies of letters by directly lifting ink from the page) and then assembled letter books, bound volumes containing copies of letters both sent and received; similarly, Thomas Jefferson made use of the 'Polygraph' letter-copying machine from 1806 until his death.[2] More simply, George Sand kept a handlist of letters sent, so that even if some letters have disappeared, we still have a clear sense of the extent of the corpus. In all these cases, we are able to reconstruct the correspondence network, even if we lack the original letters. This is not the case with Voltaire, where much is lost and we must make estimations on the basis of what has survived. He made no attempt to keep a record of the large number of letters that he sent, and we can infer that he kept copies of his letters only in exceptional cases, for example when he thought that he might later want to publish a particular letter.

Voltaire certainly never envisaged publishing his correspondence as a whole. Only a small number of his letters were published in his lifetime, in journals or books, sometimes at his instigation, sometimes with his tacit approval, and at other times without his knowledge or even, when the publication of his letters was intended to damage his reputation, against his will. The general public was well aware of the fact that he corresponded with Frederick II and later with Catherine II, and these high-profile epistolary relationships with monarchs formed an important element of his public persona. At the other end of the scale, Voltaire's letters are often presented as models worthy of imitation for instance in Louis Philipon de La Madelaine's letter manual *Modèles de lettres sur différents sujets*, first published in 1761, and continuously reprinted into the early nineteenth century. Mostly citing letters by French writers no longer living, such as Mme de Sévigné and the abbé de Chaulieu, Philipon in addition includes some ten exemplary letters by Voltaire, who is thus consecrated as a living classic. It seems fair to conclude that Voltaire was celebrated in his lifetime as a great letter-writer but that his correspondence was not acclaimed as a single entity. The idea of a writer publishing their collected letters is very much a modern notion. The 'correspondence' understood as an integrated and organised collection of all his letters is not something that Voltaire would have

---

[2] See www.mountvernon.org/library/digitalhistory/digital-encyclopedia/article/copy-press and www.monticello.org/site/research-and-collections/polygraph.

wanted to publish; it is by no means certain he would even have understood the concept. It was only after his death that a group of men of letters, all of them ideologically in sympathy with Voltaire, decided to 'create' his correspondence. This is a masterpiece that happened by accident.

Creating the Corpus

During Voltaire's lifetime, his letters were published only sporadically. The first attempt to assemble the correspondence was made by the editors of the so-called Kehl edition (1784–9), the first complete publication of his works produced after Voltaire's death. They managed to assemble a corpus of some 4,500 letters, printed in eighteen volumes, which they present deliberately as a monument designed to honour the great man. Subsequent nineteenth-century editions of Voltaire's complete works – and there were many during the years of the Restoration – followed the broad pattern set by Kehl, though they continued to add new letters as they came to light. Adrien Beuchot's edition (1829–34) included for the first time letters written to, as well as by, Voltaire, a key innovation that introduced a more sophisticated understanding of his epistolary exchanges and the sense of a network; this two-way correspondence has been retained ever since. By the time of Louis Moland's edition (1877–85), the corpus of Voltaire letters had grown to around 10,500, and further discoveries continued to be made in the course of the twentieth century. André Delattre catalogued these (1952) and helped pave the way for Theodore Besterman, who produced not one but two complete editions of Voltaire's complete correspondence. The first appeared between 1953 and 1964 and was immediately followed by the second, which Besterman rashly describes as 'definitive'. It was this revised edition, appearing in fifty-one volumes between 1968 and 1977, that gave us our modern corpus of 21,222 letters.

Current research on Voltaire's correspondence continues to uncover new letters, and even new correspondents.[3] Some of these discoveries are substantial, like the group of some 130 letters from Voltaire to his niece, Marie-Louise Denis, dating from between 1737 and 1744, while other important collections are known to be in private hands and will, it is hoped, eventually enter the public domain. Such research tends to rely heavily on serendipity, or serendipity now assisted by the increasing availability of online auction catalogues. It might also be possible to envisage a more systematic way of identifying lacunae in the existing corpus. Use of the simple word search function, for example applied to the subscription, has been employed successfully to identify the hitherto unknown addressee of certain letters (Cronk, 2016a). We are already aware of

---

[3] See www.voltaire.ox.ac.uk/about-voltaire/voltaires-correspondence.

some gaping absences, like the letters exchanged between Voltaire and Émilie Du Châtelet, presumed to have been destroyed, and we might be able to identify other correspondents, even if their letters have not survived. It has recently come to light that the Duc d'Uzès kept copies of all his exchanges with Voltaire, and this allows us to reconstruct in full one small subset of the correspondence network (Cronk, 2016b); this example is perhaps rare but may not be unique. Such investigations could in due course help us compute an estimate of the true size of Voltaire's epistolary corpus. Our statistical analyses would look very different if we had a better sense of what proportion of the whole the present extant corpus represents.

1.3 Voltaire's Correspondence as Network

The second Besterman print edition of Voltaire's correspondence was included as part of the Mellon-funded *Electronic Enlightenment* (*EE*) project, begun in 2001 at the Voltaire Foundation and launched as a commercial product by Oxford University Press in 2009.[4] The full text and scholarly apparatus (including Besterman's editorial notes and variants) of each letter was transcribed from the print edition and encoded in XML (extensible markup language) and then linked to a common metadata scheme (people, places, names, etc.) as part of *EE*'s initial data entry project (Cronk, 2020). The existence of this new dataset instantly transformed the possibilities of research into Voltaire's correspondence. In addition to Voltaire's, *EE* includes other eighteenth-century correspondences, in both English and French, including those of John Locke, David Hume, and Jean-Jacques Rousseau, always taken from the best available critical edition: the guiding spirit of the project was to use the web to recreate the 'web' of eighteenth-century correspondence. While *EE*'s texts remain under copyright restrictions, its metadata has been made available to researchers freely since 2010, most notably as the founding dataset of the *Mapping the Republic of Letters* project at Stanford (Edelstein, 2020).

The centrality of correspondence networks to the flourishing of Enlightenment thought and exchange has become a significant area of scholarly interest. In the *Encyclopédie*, Diderot adopts a somewhat high-minded view of such networks, seeing them as potentially fostering the disinterested exchange of information between people of different ranks in different places:

> Il ne seroit pas inutile d'établir des correspondances dans les lieux principaux du monde lettré, & je ne doute point qu'on n'y réussît. On s'instruira des usages, des coûtumes, des productions, des travaux, des machines, &c. si on

---

[4] See http://e-enlightenment.com/.

ne néglige personne, & si l'on a pour tous ce degré de considération que l'on doit à l'homme desintéressé qui veut se rendre utile. (Diderot, 1755, p. 645)

It would be useful to establish correspondence exchanges in the principal centres of the cultivated world, and I am in no doubt that this could work. We shall learn about usages, customs, productions, projects, machines, etc. if we include everybody and treat everyone with the consideration that is due to the disinterested man who wants to be useful.

In order truly to recreate the Republic of Letters, it would be desirable to track the exchanges of many scholars, including the so-called 'lesser' figures who worked in provincial centres, like the Avignon physician Esprit Calvet (Brockliss, 2002), or his friend the botanist and archaeologist Jean-François Séguier, based in Nîmes.[5] There is therefore huge potential for future research as and when *EE* is able to extend its current practice of including archival print editions of major figures to include born-digital editions of the 'lesser' figures – who are, of course, in their scholarly practice more typical of Enlightenment authors than the small number of great writers who, by definition, are necessarily exceptional. Looking to the future, we now begin to have the materials to set about re-creating, as it were from the inside, the Republic of Letters, a concept much discussed but still poorly understood (Hotson & Wallnig, 2019). A future goal, obviously, would be to create cross-searchable datasets so that we could map the network of Voltaire's correspondence in the context of the broader European, and later American, network of Enlightenment correspondences. Digital resources have the potential to provide powerful tools for the intellectual historian, and the challenge now is to find the most appropriate ways of applying new digital methods to advance Enlightenment intellectual history (Edelstein, 2016).

It is also important to focus on the networks of individual letter writers, and the network of every great author has its own particularities (Clemit, 2019). Digital researchers can already, thanks to *EE*, focus on the Voltaire correspondence network as a single entity, and the earliest initiative to make use of *EE* explored the possibilities of mapping the Voltaire epistolary network. Under Dan Edelstein's leadership, the *Mapping the Republic of Letters* project at Stanford has helped us to visualise this network.[6] We can now view Voltaire's correspondence as a geographical whole (see Fig. 1.2) or by chronological period, or we may compare, say, the correspondence networks of Voltaire and Locke (Edelstein, 2019).

Sometimes the results are predictable (which is reassuring), as when we find that Paris seems to be the hub of the Enlightenment, and sometimes not, as when Edelstein points out that Voltaire's letters to England are far fewer in number than we might have expected, given the standard narrative about the role of

---

[5] See www.seguier.org.   [6] See http://republicofletters.stanford.edu/.

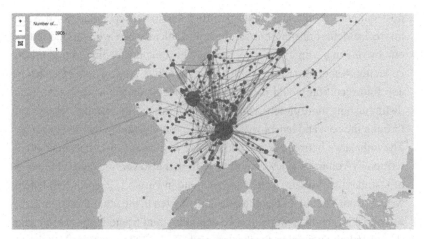

Figure 1.2 Voltaire's correspondence network, visualised in Palladio

England and France in the growth of the European Enlightenment (Edelstein & Kassabova, 2018). A natural extension of this research is to use the Voltaire corpus to explore the possibilities of social network analysis, and this is already yielding significant results concerning the social profile of Voltaire's correspondents (Comsa et al., 2016); we are still only at the very beginning of what is possible in the digital exploration of epistolary networks.

It is crucial in conducting these analyses to reflect on what precisely it is we are mapping when we visualise Voltaire's correspondence network. The Voltairean corpus poses a formidable challenge to the interpreter: many letters are missing, because they were destroyed or have been lost, while some of the letters in the present corpus are rewritten versions of the originals, and perhaps even forgeries. So in order to better explore this network, we need first to understand better how it came into being.

The Imbalanced Corpus

A striking feature of the epistolary corpus assembled by Besterman is its profoundly lopsided composition. The letters are far more numerous in the later decades of Voltaire's life than in the earlier ones, and the letters written by Voltaire (over 15,000) vastly outnumber those written to him (around 6,000). In trying to understand just how this lopsidedness came to be, three factors should be borne in mind:

1. The first is the question of definition, what we may call the laundry list problem. Besterman's criteria for defining a letter are remarkably vague, and he tends to include in his edition everything, from letters sent through the

post to literary works such as journal articles written in epistolary form. Such imprecise definitions are not as much a problem when we read the letters one by one in a printed volume, but they become misleading in a digitised collection where we are attempting distant reading. An essential next step in any future edition would be to attribute category labels to each text, thus distinguishing more clearly than at present between, for example, letters sent through the post and letters written for print publication in the first instance.

2. The imbalance between active and passive correspondence, between letters written by Voltaire and letters written to him, is also very marked. In the case of Damilaville, Voltaire's stalwart helpmate in Paris, *EE* records 576 letters written from Voltaire to Damilaville and only ten in the other direction. Or if we take d'Argental, a highly placed and influential friend in the capital who shared Voltaire's passion for theatre, we have 1,209 letters from Voltaire to d'Argental, and only forty-six in the other direction. Of course, these statistics describe not the number of letters actually written but the number of letters that have survived. French epistolary etiquette (then as now) emphasises the need to acknowledge receipt of any letter, so broadly speaking, we should expect to find, for each correspondent, approximately the same number of letters in each direction. We can infer that many of Voltaire's correspondents carefully preserved his letters; Voltaire himself, on the other hand, once he had replied to a letter, seems very often to have discarded it.

3. There is a significant difference, too, between the number of letters written in the early years of Voltaire's life and the far greater number surviving from later years. In part this evolution must reflect a reality: as he grew older and became increasingly involved in a wider range of activities, there were simply more letters to be written. But in part this disparity reflects the reasons for which letters were kept; when Voltaire was young and little known, his letters were easily discarded; as he grew more famous, the temptation to hold on to an example of the great man's writing became increasingly irresistible. Antoine Lilti describes Voltaire as the first modern celebrity (Lilti, 2014, chap. 1), and celebrity is clearly one key factor in explaining the distorted shape of this epistolary corpus: the more famous he became, the more zealously his correspondents sought out and preserved his letters.

How Was the Corpus Constituted?

Given that Voltaire himself did not consistently collect his letters for publication, how exactly did the editors of the Kehl edition assemble their epistolary corpus? There are broadly three sources for their material:

1. *Letters published in Voltaire's lifetime.* On occasion, Voltaire chose to publish a letter in a journal or in one of his printed works. In other cases, letters were published without his apparent authorisation – though the extent of his complicity in the publication of his letters is sometimes hard to assess, as in the case of the letters that appeared in the *Correspondance littéraire* after 1763. As Voltaire's fame grew, he must have realised that the risk of his letters being published was all the greater, and this in turn influenced the style and content of certain of his letters. On occasion the publication of Voltaire's letters by a third party was done with clearly hostile intent (and in these cases, the text was often falsified for polemical reasons). As a result, Voltaire struggled increasingly to maintain control over the dissemination of his letters.

2. *Letters collected by the Kehl editors.* The editors of the Kehl edition sought out letters still in the possession of Voltaire's correspondents, but this was no easy task, so in addition they advertised in 1780 for owners of Voltaire's letters to come forward.

3. *Letters left by Voltaire and inherited by the Kehl editors.* A certain number of letters or copies of letters survived in Voltaire's *Nachlass* and did not go to St Petersburg with the rest of his papers and library, acquired by Catherine II shortly after his death. The Kehl editors inherited these in due course, after an edition planned by the publisher Charles-Joseph Panckoucke had come to nothing, and clearly these letters constitute a significant part of their corpus. Voltaire informs one of his correspondents that he destroyed letters received on a regular basis, so what he left behind is presumably to some extent what he chose to leave behind, and it seems improbable, given his deliberate attempts to control his literary corpus in other areas, that he would have left much to chance in the manuscripts that he allowed to survive.

The Character of Voltaire's Epistolary Corpus

This brief survey of how the Kehl epistolary corpus came into being suggests that it is hardly a 'neutral' cross-section of Voltaire's letters. At least with regard to the letters preserved by Voltaire, it would seem that what has survived must be a carefully controlled set of letters preserved by Voltaire to show him in the best possible light. This is all the more interesting when we remember the ideological assumptions of the Kehl editors themselves, who insist that their purpose in creating the correspondence is to display the character of Voltaire in the most positive way. The 'Avis' inviting members of the public to share their Voltaire manuscripts urges them to contribute to perfecting 'le monument qui va s'élever à la gloire de ce beau génie' (Voltaire, 2017, p. 547) (the monument that will be raised to the glory of this great genius), and the same desire to glorify Voltaire's genius is expressed by the Kehl editors in their preface:

> Enfin le recueil des lettres complètera l'édition. Mais ces lettres seront choisies: c'est-à-dire qu'on n'imprimera que celles qui paraîtront dignes du public, soit en elles-mêmes, soit par les particularités qu'elles renferment, les circonstances où elles ont été écrites, les lumières qu'elles donnent sur l'âme et le caractère d'un homme vraiment unique, et digne par son génie et la singularité de ses talents d'être pour les philosophes un objet d'étude, comme il est un objet d'admiration pour tous les hommes impartiaux et éclairés. (Voltaire, 1784, vol. I, p. viii)

> Finally, the collection of letters will complete the edition. But these letters will be selected, that is to say that we shall only print those which seem worthy of the public, either in themselves, or in the particular details they contain, the circumstances in which they were written, the insights they give into the mind and character of a truly unique man, worthy by his genius and by his particular talents to be an object of study for philosophers, as he is an object of admiration for all impartial and enlightened men.

To a greater or lesser extent, all editors of Voltaire's letters fall into this hagiographical trap, but it is not clear that the Kehl editors were aware of the circularity of their argument. As editors we can only edit what we have before us, but we can try at least to show an awareness that the corpus is in part shaped by the controlling hand of Voltaire himself.

Another factor to be borne in mind is the ever-present tension between private and public in these letters (as in other correspondences of the period): some are clearly personal communications, some are private communications designed to be shared with close friends, while others are clearly composed with the idea that they might circulate in manuscript copy or even end up being printed. This leads to a question concerning the accuracy, or rather inaccuracy, of the texts that have come down to us. In the case of letters published in Voltaire's lifetime, we can never be entirely confident, in the absence of the autograph, that they have not been revised or rewritten for publication. Moreover, the manuscript descriptions in the Besterman edition are often minimal and do not always help us to distinguish between letters as they were communicated in private and letters as they were prepared for print.

The letters written to Marie-Louise Denis from Potsdam in the early 1750s describing life at the Prussian court are some of the most harshly ironic in the entire correspondence, and for obvious reasons they have been much anthologised; it is only since the completion of Besterman's 'definitive' edition of the correspondence that we have understood that these letters are not in fact the originals (the evidence of the autographs having been destroyed, it seems), but rather rewritten versions designed to ridicule Frederick. Voltaire's plan to publish these as a sort of epistolary novel, perhaps under the title *Paméla*, was shelved, but the rewritten manuscript collection of letters was carefully preserved. This example may well not be unique: how many other 'rewritten' letters still lie undiscovered in Besterman's edition? In cases where we suspect Voltaire of rewriting and 'improving' an original, it might be possible to devise clustering techniques that would aid us to distinguish on stylistic grounds groups and subgroups of letters within the overall corpus.

The Kehl editors who, as we have seen, are the effective inventors of Voltaire's correspondence, say little about how their corpus was assembled, but they are explicit about their editorial interventions in the preface quoted above: 'Les lettres qui pourraient blesser des personnes vivantes ont été sévèrement retranchées' (Voltaire, 1784, vol. I, p. viii) (The letters which could embarrass living persons have been severely edited). In other words, they admit to selecting only letters 'worthy of the public' and confess to censoring details in the interests of protecting living persons – how many scurrilous details must have been lost. Even Adrien Beuchot, in many respects the greatest Voltaire editor of the nineteenth century, in his edition of the complete works limits the notion of 'complete' to what is 'interesting':

> Quelque jaloux que j'aie été d'enrichir l'édition confiée à mes soins, je déclare n'avoir pas admis toutes les lettres qui me sont connues [...]. Je n'ai admis [...] dans la collection, que les lettres qui m'ont paru avoir quelque intérêt. La *Correspondance* de Voltaire n'est déjà que trop volumineuse. Que serait-ce donc si l'on avait toutes ses lettres? (Voltaire, 1829–34, vol. 51, p. vii)

> Despite my keenness to enrich the edition that has been entrusted to me, I admit not having included all the letters known to me [...]. I have included [...] in the collection only the letters that seemed to me to possess some interest. Voltaire's *Correspondence* is already too bulky. What would it be like if we had all his letters?

More recent editors have happily been less discriminating, preferring to include every letter that came to hand; but many of the manuscripts known to the Kehl editors and to Beuchot must now be lost without trace.

Nothing in this epistolary corpus can be taken quite at face value. It is always tempting to think of a letter by Voltaire as the spontaneous outpouring of his feelings and ideas, but such a naïve reading is rarely possible in his case (or indeed in the case of any author). There is much evidence suggesting that Voltaire exercised control over the corpus, insofar as he was able, so that in the end, we read what he wanted us to read. Moreover, it is often not possible to

Figure 1.3 Voltaire stamp

distinguish between an autograph letter and a rewritten version of it, and we have evidence that the text of many of these letters is unstable and unreliable. A Voltaire letter should be read and interpreted like any other literary text of Voltaire's, as a literary performance.

A stamp produced by the French Post in 1998 depicts Voltaire writing letters with both hands (see Fig. 1.3). This charming image certainly captures the sense of frenetic speed with which he composed, though it is not clear that an ambidextrous letter-writer can be altogether trusted. Voltaire's correspondence network is full of traps, and we are far from having understood all his tricks. New critical approaches to the corpus may yet prove extremely revealing.

1.4 Digital Readings of Voltaire's Correspondence

It may well be argued that correspondence collections, especially those having the scope and scale of Voltaire's, only reach their full potential once digitised and connected to other similar digital artefacts. This is in essence the idea behind the *EE* project (Cronk & McNamee, 2005). Once assembled, these sorts of federated digital resources can become invaluable research tools across a host of disciplines in the humanities, from intellectual and book history, the history of art, and philosophy, to science and technology studies, among others. Techniques such as network analysis, developed for the most part in the social sciences, are particularly well suited to the sociological and prosopographical exploration of correspondence datasets and their associated metadata (Edmondson & Edelstein, 2019). But what, if anything, can the *literary critic* glean from such quantitative approaches to what are often large and overly mundane collections of epistolary documents? And, more generally, how can digital modes of 'reading' – understood here in its broadest sense as the fundamental activity of literary scholarship and criticism – advance, and perhaps change, our understanding of writers such as Voltaire and their processes of literary creation and diffusion?

Much ink has been spilled in literary studies around the term 'distant reading' since its coining by Franco Moretti some two decades ago (Moretti, 2000). Yet 'distant' methods for conducting literary research go back much further, at least to the philologists of the nineteenth century, if not to the first concordances of the Scholastics in the thirteenth (Underwood, 2017). Our intention here is not to enter into these larger debates but rather to affirm the simple postulate that digital collections – whether composed of letters, literary works, or historical documents – can, and should, enable multiple reading strategies and interpretative points of entry. It is important in this age of mass digitisation and big data that digital literary studies, a subfield of the digital humanities, continue to offer inroads for traditional critical practices while at the same time opening up new, unexplored avenues that take full advantage of the affordances of the digital. Alongside the asking of traditional literary-critical questions in new ways – benefitting from economies of both scale and speed – digital humanities methods should also *generate new research questions* from historical content, so providing interpretive frameworks that would have been impossible in a predigital world. Our goal in this essay is to provide just such a framework for Voltaire.

The size and complexity of Voltaire's correspondence make it an almost ideal corpus for testing the two dominant modes of (digital) literary analysis: on the one hand, 'distant' approaches to the corpus as a whole and its relationship to a larger literary culture; on the other, fine-grained analyses of individual letters and passages that serve to contextualise the particular in terms of the general, and vice versa. The core question at the heart of this essay is thus one that remains largely untreated in the wider world: how can we use digital 'reading' methods – both close and distant – to explore and better understand a literary object as complex and multifaceted as Voltaire's correspondence? Moving from simple techniques such as lexical matching, text encoding, and keyword searches to more complex algorithmically produced analyses based on sequence alignment and machine-learning approaches, such as topic modelling, we aim to demonstrate the viability of digital humanities methods for literary studies when tackling this sort of large and unwieldy textual corpus.

No corpus exists in a vacuum, however, no matter how large it may be; and the ability to bring other digital resources into conversation with Voltaire's letters is perhaps one of the most innovative aspects of the current study. Thanks to the authors' long-standing collaborative relationship with, on the one hand, the Voltaire Foundation at the University of Oxford,[7] and, on the other, the University of Chicago's ARTFL Project,[8] we were able to marshal an impressive collection of datasets in order to construct the experiments that follow. Primary among these are *TOUT Voltaire*, an open-access database of all of Voltaire's writings, drawn primarily from the Voltaire Foundation's *Complete Works of Voltaire* project as well as the best available editions from the nineteenth century;[9] and ARTFL-Frantext, a subscription-based corpus of some 3,500 French-language texts made available for research purposes by the ARTFL Project.[10] This same spirit of federating eighteenth-century digital resources led us in 2018 to establish the Voltaire Lab, a virtual space for digital humanities research on the Enlightenment, and to make available to researchers *TV2* (*TOUT Voltaire2*), a database that makes search and exploration across the entirety of Voltaire's written output – works and letters combined – possible for the first time.[11] Building on these various efforts, plans are currently underway for *Digital Voltaire*, a scholarly digital edition of Voltaire's complete works and letters that will, hopefully, complete and complement its print predecessor.

Each of the following sections of this Element thus makes use of the above resources to some degree and relies on various forms of digital editing, corpus and text analysis to address one specific aspect of Voltaire's correspondence; and each serves to demonstrate the potential of digital techniques to enhance our understanding of the epistolary corpus as a whole. Section 2 deals with Voltaire's signatures and the names and games he enacts when signing off his letters. According to the conventions of French epistolary writing, Voltaire rarely names his addressee at the beginning of a letter. However, at the end of letters, particularly writing to friends, he demonstrates limitless ingenuity in the way he shapes his valedictions and varies the form of his signature. Given the sheer number of letters he wrote, a full description of the richness and breadth of Voltaire's signatory practice can only be understood fully at scale and by way of digital analysis. By leveraging the structural encoding that undergirds most

---

[7] See www.voltaire.ox.ac.uk/.   [8] See https://artfl-project.uchicago.edu/.

[9] See https://artfl-project.uchicago.edu/tout-voltaire

[10] See https://artfl-project.uchicago.edu/content/artfl-frantext. The Frantext database is the result of collaboration between the CNRS in France and the University of Chicago, which aimed to leverage the corpus of canonical French literary texts begun in the 1950s in order to complete the *Trésor de la langue française* French dictionary. Since 1981 the American and French versions of 'Frantext' have evolved differently. Today, ARTFL-Frantext contains over 3,500 literary and historical works from the thirteenth to mid-twentieth centuries, drawn primarily from modern editions.

[11] On the Voltaire Lab and *TV2*, see www.voltaire.ox.ac.uk/about-voltaire/voltaire-lab and www.voltaire.ox.ac.uk/news/blog/voltaire-lab-new-digital-research-tools-and-resources.

digital editions today, we identify, extract, and analyse all of Voltaire's signatures included in the over 15,000 letters he wrote or dictated. The creativity of these signatures is a key part of Voltaire's self-fashioning as he constructs individual relationships with important correspondents, and it is also remarkable testimony to the fantasy of his improvisations, even in apparently 'private' works. The variety and breadth of these naming conventions is astounding and is a subject that remains largely unexplored beyond a few notable cases.

Section 3 deals with Voltaire as wordsmith, a writer who consciously invents new words and experiments with them through his correspondence networks. Traditionally, critics have described Voltaire as an arch-classicist who adheres rigorously to the norms and precepts of seventeenth-century French classicism. While this is undoubtedly true – Voltaire, along with many of his contemporaries, considered that the French language reached a point of perfection in the late 1600s – he is nonetheless an innovator in the abundant creation of neologisms. This is an aspect of his literary style that has been insufficiently recognised in contemporary scholarship. Here, corpus analysis tools, coupled with available lexicographical digital resources, allow us to consider Voltaire's aesthetic of lexical innovation. In so doing, we can test the hypothesis that Voltaire uses the correspondence as a laboratory in which he can experiment with new formulations, ideas, and words, some of which then pass into his printed, canonical works.

Any reader of Voltaire's letters will immediately be struck by the frequency of his literary quotations. Section 4 aims to explore this phenomenon through the use of sequence alignment algorithms – similar to those used in bioinformatics to sequence genetic data – to identify similar or shared passages. Using the ARTFL-Frantext database of French literature as a comparison dataset,[12] we attempt a detailed quantification and description of French literary quotations contained in Voltaire's correspondence. These citations, taken together, give us a more comprehensive understanding of Voltaire's literary culture and his practice as a literary critic and provide invaluable insights into his rhetoric of intertextuality. For example, there is a preponderance of references to writers from Voltaire's revered 'century of Louis XIV', notably to the playwrights Corneille and Racine, who inspire his own theatrical works, making quotation in many ways a vehicle for literary creation.

Quotations in Latin also abound in Voltaire's letters, evidence of another key element of his humanist culture. Section 5 attempts to understand Voltaire's use of Latin quotations as a particular form of sociability insofar as their use is restricted to a particular set of correspondents. Many of these quotes are drawn

---

[12] https://artfl-project.uchicago.edu/content/artfl-frantext.

from predictably famous authors (Horace, Virgil, Ovid) – whom Voltaire would have memorised while in school – while others come from lesser poets, like Manilius.

Again using sequence alignment, we identify all the Latin quotations in Voltaire's letters by comparison with the Packard Humanities Institute's collection of digital Latin texts. Once analysed, it becomes clear that these passages, which Voltaire often seems to be quoting from memory, grant us further insights into the full extent of his erudition and into the ways in which he deploys quotations as a rhetorical device. We wondered how discriminating Voltaire was in his use of Latin quotation in his letters, also bearing in mind that Latin was normally the exclusive province of men's education (with notable but rare exceptions, such as Émilie Du Châtelet). By examining those correspondents who receive Latin quotations as a group and assigning to them social and intellectual categories established by colleagues working at Stanford, and taking gender specificity into account, we are able to establish clear networks of Latin usage throughout the correspondence.

Beyond the specific experiments conducted in the sections outlined above, our Section 6 explores the various ways in which the digital edition of Voltaire's correspondence naturally opens itself to other avenues of future research. The print edition, for example, leaves some eighty-eight correspondents unidentified; stylometry, network analysis, and other digital methods can probably be used to fill in some of these gaps in authorship. Stylometric analysis can also be used to explore Voltaire's status as an author and public figure, identifying patterns of stylistic expression used with certain groups of correspondents (men of letters, for instance) as opposed to personal or transactional letters. Moving from the simple to the sophisticated – from the closest to the most distant – we can use machine learning techniques, such as topic modelling, to identify and categorise the predominant themes and topical shape of the correspondence, generating links between letters and correspondents that would have been impossible to follow otherwise. In the future, conceptual space might be explored using new linguistic models generated by neural networks, a branch of artificial intelligence. By examining Voltaire's word embedding (i.e., the relative space that his words occupy compared to larger eighteenth-century datasets) we will be able to generate conceptual maps of Voltaire's language usage in the letters, tracing the evolution of concepts over time, and linking them with historical events, political campaigns, and philosophical debates.

These more complex digital techniques move us in many respects to a point of maximum distance from Voltaire's letters, where individual texts are no longer readable in any real, human sense. But our contention is that as alienating as this distance may seem, the new vistas and perspectives they offer on the entirety of the correspondence provide insights and pathways that can only be understood at the human scale of close and considered interpretation. While single letters obviously benefit from close reading techniques and traditional hermeneutics, the correspondence as a whole – understood as a complex, incomplete, and at times intractable literary object – can gain enormously from distant readings, be they sociological, quantitative, or computational. This is not to say, however, that this new literary object is somehow free from the hermeneutic circle; far from it. The next generation of literary scholars will need interpretive frameworks that can take into account both ends of the close/distant spectrum, where the two forms of analysis become mutually enriching. In the end, Voltaire's correspondence is undoubtedly one of his greatest literary accomplishments – but arguably one that becomes fully legible only with the use of digital resources and methods. It is in this spirit that we offer the following readings.

2 Names

2.1 Introduction

Voltaire was not, of course, called Voltaire. The man born François-Marie Arouet was a great inventor of names, and 'Voltaire' was his greatest fictional creation. Voltaire in turn invented other names, and while his use of pseudonyms in his published works is well known, the presence of this naming mania in the correspondence seems not to have been studied. One stark statistic to begin with: in the 15,723 letters at our disposal, Voltaire uses 586 different signatures. These signatures in turn become an integral part of the letter-writing process, and, as we shall see, the decision to sign (or not sign) a letter contributes to its function as a fundamentally 'social text' (McGann, 1991, 2006; McKenzie, 1999).

It is perhaps a good idea to recall, at the outset of this section, the rhetorical structure of a letter, which may be defined by a set of essential elements:

1. heading
2. salutation
3. body of the letter
4. subscription (or leave-taking)
5. signature
6. superscription (external)

These discrete elements are broadly common to letters both of the eighteenth century and of the twenty-first. And, it is worth adding, they lend themselves easily to being tagged in an electronic edition. A full digital edition of a letter

can be a powerful tool for analysing the structure of a body of correspondence –
and, in fact, the TEI (Text Encoding Initiative) XML encoding standard mirrors
many of these same elements ('heading', 'salutation', 'body', etc.) as here:

> <salute>To all courteous mindes, that will voutchsafe the readinge.</salute>
> [...]
> <signed>Thine to command <name>Humph. Moseley</name> </signed>[13]

While not technically encoded in TEI, the XML markup used by *EE* includes
just this sort of structural tagging. By being given access to the source XML files
of Voltaire's correspondence – made available by *EE* and the Voltaire
Foundation – we were able, for the purposes of this experiment, to extract all
of Voltaire's subscriptions and signatures directly from the encoded texts, for
example:

> votre très humble et très obéissant serviteur
>
> <class="signoff">Voltaire

We are asking two sets of interrelated questions in this section: first, what are
these 586 signatures? How does Voltaire play with naming in his letters? What
are the implications of this playfulness to his interlocutors, to the reader?
Second, how can digitised collections and their enhanced search and retrieval
capabilities aid in this sort of research? Beyond searching, how can the
digitisation of a letter, or collection of letters, change our traditional approach
to the critical edition – that is, due to their inherently 'social' nature, how
might letters (or networks of letters) be tagged differently from other textual
artefacts, and what are the broader implications of this 'digital turn' in
scholarly editing?

2.2 Voltaire's Signatures

Conventional Signatures

Voltaire's earliest letters are signed 'Arouet' (D1, 1704; D2, 1711) or 'A***'
(D7, 1713).[14] He is still signing 'Arouet' in April 1718 (D58); then in June of
the same year, he signs a letter to Lord Ashburnham 'Arouet de Voltaire' (D62;
see note on this letter); and from late 1718, aged twenty-four, he starts to sign
'Voltaire' (D70). He uses his invented name 'Voltaire' in full in slightly formal

---

[13] See the TEI Special Interest Group on Correspondence here: https://wiki.tei-c.org/index.php/
SIG:Correspondence.

[14] To refer to Voltaire's letters, we are following standard practice here by using the numbering of
the second Besterman print edition, where each letter number is preceded by a D (for 'definitive'), for example D123.

contexts, or when addressing someone he does not know well: in writing to a local mayor (D9379) and to the poet Le Brun (D9382), he opens 'Monsieur' and concludes, 'Monsieur, Votre très humble et très obéissant serviteur, Voltaire' (Sir, your most humble and obedient servant). More rarely, he signs with an abridged form: 'Volt.' (D9484).

And on grand occasions, when he wants to impress, he signs with his court title: 'Voltaire gentilhomme ordinaire du roy' (D9123), which he reworks in English when writing to Lord Lyttelton, 'Voltaire / gentleman of the King's chamber / at my castle of Fernex in Burgundy' (D9231).

Far more frequently, however, when writing to friends and colleagues, Voltaire signs off with a single letter: 'V'. The statistics are telling: out of a total of 15,723 letters by Voltaire, we find:

'V.':	5,456 occurrences (34.7%)
'Voltaire':	2,087 occurrences (13.3%)
'Volt.':	61 occurrences (0.4%)

'V.' is therefore more than twice as frequent as 'Voltaire' and 'Volt.'; indeed 'V.' is the signature in over a third of all the letters.

Unconventional Signatures

These results show that over half the letters are *not* signed by one of these three 'conventional' forms of his name (Voltaire, Volt., V.), and these unsigned letters are addressed to a wide range of correspondents.[15] Often Voltaire invents a name. Elsewhere in his works, pseudonyms are deployed to conceal, or to pretend to conceal, his identity, but concealing one's identity in a letter – unless it is a poison pen letter – does not make much sense. Voltaire cultivates invented names in his correspondence, not to hide his identity but to project it, and the invented personae, or masks, assume a bewildering range of different forms.

Descriptive Names: Inventions and Variations

Among what we have called the unconventional signatures, there is a plethora of invention, and Voltaire exercises considerable playfulness inventing and

---

[15] The text of many of the letters in the Besterman edition is taken from a manuscript copy or a later print edition rather than from the autograph, so it is always possible that inaccuracies in the transcription of the signature have crept in. Even if such inaccuracies exist, however, they would not significantly alter the results presented here.

reinventing his signature. To begin with, he can take a conventional signature and extend it:

'le suisse V.' (the Swiss V.) (D9856)
'Le Suisse Voltaire' (The Swiss Voltaire) (D9566)
'le vieux suisse V.' (the old Swiss V.) (D9608)
'Le vieux suisse Voltaire' (The old Swiss Voltaire) (D9567)
'Le petit suisse V.' (The little Swiss V.) (D9618)
'L'hermite V.' (The hermit V.) (D9194)
'Le vieil hermite V.' (The old hermit V.) (D16093)
'Votre contemporain V.' (V. your contemporary) (D9611)
'le vieux de la montagne V.' (the old man of the mountain V.) (D18585)
'Le vieux solitaire du mont Jura V.' (The old solitary of Mt Jura V.)
    (D18686)

One way of creating complicity with his correspondents is by the use of Latin (we shall return to this), and to his publisher Cramer, he is sometimes 'Tuus V.' (Your V.) (D9264).

The next step in this process of invention is to maintain a descriptive element, while dropping the name altogether: the signature now becomes a periphrasis rather than a name:

'Du vieux Suisse' (From the old Swiss) (D9328)
'L'ermite de Ferney' (The hermit of Ferney) (D9559)
'le vieux mouton broutant au pied des Alpes' (the old sheep grazing at the
    foot of the Alps) (D9791)

Voltaire deploys names to create different personae, like that of the old man, the valetudinarian at death's door (Cotoni, 1995). These descriptive signatures are especially typical of Voltaire the 'patriarch', that is to say, of the period after 1760, when he established himself at Ferney, adjacent to Geneva but on French soil, as Europe's most celebrated living writer. His signatures become a powerful means of projecting an authorial posture – in letters written between 1769 and 1773, for example, certain themes are recurrent. There are 325 signatures based on 'vieux' (old), as in 'Le vieillard des Alpes' (The old man of the Alps) (D16071), 'le pauvre viéillard' (the poor old man) (D16072), and even extending to English, and 'the old man of Ferney' (D17186), 'the old invalid of Ferney' (D17188). Voltaire also plays up his isolation, and we find fifty-five signatures using the idea of the solitary or the hermit, as in the 'solitaire de Ferney' (D15664) or 'le vieil hermite de Ferney' (D16510). And to add to the drama of his isolation, Voltaire adds allusions to the mountains that surround his home: there are nineteen signatures that refer to the mountains, and twelve referring to the Alps, as in the 'pauvre vieillard des montagnes' (poor old man of the mountains) (D16026) or 'le vieil hermite du mont Jura' (the old hermit of Mount Jura) (D17035). Voltaire is a valetudinarian, and there are no fewer than 220 signatures containing the word 'malade' (sick), as in 'le pauvre malade' (the poor invalid) (D16724) or the 'vieux malade de Ferney' (old invalid of Ferney) (D16315). In the year 1771, Voltaire's concern with his health is especially focussed on his failing eyesight, and ten signatures are constructed around the persona of the 'aveugle' (the blind man), as in 'le vieux malade aveugle de Ferney' (the sick old blind man of Ferney) (D17171). Of course, any and every combination of the above is possible, as in 'le vieux radoteur aveugle entre un lac et une montagne couverte de neige' (the blind old babbler between a lake and a snow-covered mountain) (D17251).

Voltaire's inventions cover all aspects of his personality – this writer toys modestly with the idea of being a librarian, 'le bibliothécaire' (D17190), and even a printer, signing with the name 'Guillemet' (Quotation Mark – a genuine French name, so more plausible in French than in English) (D1606) and even 'Guillemet tipografe' (Quotation Mark the typographer) (D15657). A long-running joke with certain choice correspondents is to posture as a man of the Church, and we find twenty-three occurrences each of 'Capucin indigne' (unworthy Capuchin monk) (D16142) and 'frère François' (Brother Francis) (D16206). The signature 'Cucufin et frère Roch de Pediculis capucins dignes' (D16029) is untranslatable – suffice it to say that the names of the two 'worthy Capuchin monks' are calqued on the word 'cul' (arse). Voltaire also adopts the personae of animals, variously as 'le rat des Alpes' (the rat of the Alps) (D10798), 'la Marmotte des Alpes. V.' (the marmot of the Alps. V.) (D9147) and 'Le triste hibou de Ferney V.' (the sad owl of Ferney V.) (D20120). The invention is endless, and many personae, such as 'votre grammairien de Potsdam' (your grammarian from Potsdam), when writing to Frederick II (D8338), are one-offs, never to be repeated.

Subscription as Signature

Keith Thomas notes that the practice of address and subscription in letters in England was 'flexible' in the early modern period, 'freely adapted to fit particular circumstances' (Thomas, 1990, p. 452), and Voltaire pushes these freedoms to the limit and beyond. In letters of this period the salutation does not usually include the recipient's name (which is, of course, to be found on the outside of the letter, whether the reverse of the folded sheet itself or, later in the century, the envelope). So if the addressee need not be named within the letter itself, the writer of the letter can go one step further by also omitting his or her own name.

Writing to his friend, the doctor Thédore Tronchin, for example, Voltaire begins *in medias res*: 'Non mon cher docteur . . . ' (No, my dear doctor . . .) (D9204), as though they were in mid-conversation (which, in a sense, they were). In a similar vein, this letter ends with a subscription, 'Je vous embrasse du meilleur de mon cœur' (I embrace you with all my heart), but without a following signature, which, in a sense, is unnecessary – though fittingly enough, this letter contains Voltaire's complaint against a third party who has appropriated his (Voltaire's) name for his book.

A remarkable feature of Voltaire's correspondence is how often he simply omits to sign his letters. Of a total of 15,723 letters by him in *EE*, 8,535 have signatures; this means that 7,188 are without signature. Fully 45 per cent of Voltaire's letters therefore have no signature at all. In a strictly technical sense, we might argue that he does not need to sign his letters, because his seal, or his handwriting, or the handwriting of his secretary, would most likely have been familiar to his regular correspondents. Voltaire was famous from a young age, and after 1760 he had become a celebrity, a literary superstar, so his letters were likewise objects of celebrity, making a signature almost superfluous.

It seems clear that a great writer signs with his authorial persona and its embodiment in style. Voltaire addresses his correspondents with a voice so characterful, so individual, that to add a signature could be considered unnecessary, anticlimactic even. Voltaire names himself in the act of writing and need not sign his name. That said, in formal letters, as we saw above, he signs in a more conventional manner: not signing is an eccentricity that he reserves for his friends as a mark of intimacy. In cases where Voltaire avoids a signature entirely, it is the subscription that in effect takes its place. Thus to Thiriot, a friend from early days, he can end a letter with no signature but merely a phrase that stands as the subscription: 'Scribe, vale' (Write, farewell) (D9124).

The use of Latin in the subscription, pre-empting the need for any signature, is reserved for special friends: to Cramer, 'Vale amice' (Farewell friend) (D9574), and to Damilaville and, through him, his circle, 'Valete fratres' (Farewell brothers) (D9826). The Latin subscription is a particular feature of Voltaire's letters to Thiriot, a souvenir perhaps of the Latin classes they once shared: 'Si quid novi scribe' (Write if there's something new) (D9211), 'Vale, vive, scribe, laetare' (Farewell, live, write, enjoy) (D9449), 'Interim vale et me ama' (Meanwhile farewell and love me) (D9549). Writing to the bisexual Algarotti, Voltaire chooses the intimacy of Latin to express a flirtatious affection in a subscription with no following signature: 'Laetus sum, non validus, sed tui amantissimus' (I'm happy, not strong, but to you most loving) (D9428).

Put simply, Voltaire rewrites the rules for how to sign letters. He wrote over 1,200 letters to his close friend d'Argental, many addressed jointly to d'Argental and his wife, whom he habitually calls his 'anges' (guardian angels): there are 649 letters from Voltaire to d'Argental in which the word 'ange' occurs. So when d'Argental receives a letter beginning 'Mon arcange, que votre volonté soit faite sur le théâtre comme ailleurs' (My archangel, may your will be done, on stage as elsewhere) (D9113), he knows instantly that this address and this rewriting of the Lord's Prayer can be from one person only. The subscription is equally individual: 'Mon cher ange je vous le répète il ne me manque que de vous embrasser, mais cela me manque horriblement' (My dear angel, I repeat, the one thing I miss is to embrace you, but that I miss dreadfully). After that, it would have been entirely superfluous for Voltaire to sign his name. Voltaire is a master of the art of naming himself without signing.

2.3 Epistolary Circuits: Networks of Sociability

A third striking fact about Voltaire's naming games concerns the way he uses epistolary postures to create networks of sociability. Voltaire is remarkable at reinventing himself, and more than that, in a gesture of particular intimacy, he reinvents himself differently for each close friend. There are one-off inventions that are not returned – closed circuits, in effect. In other cases the correspondent joins in the game and bats the name back: in these cases, the exchange of epistolary codes creates complicity; a true epistolary circuit.

Voltaire as Marmot

In 1759, the duc de Choiseul addresses Voltaire as 'ma chère marmotte' (my dear marmot) (D8387). He is replying to a letter that has not come down to us, so we cannot be sure if the first use of the image is his or Voltaire's – probably the latter. Either way, the image fitted – marmots live in mountainous areas and tend to hibernate in winter – and it stuck and was used by both correspondents. Between 1759 and 1768, Choiseul writes in fifteen letters of 'Ma chère marmotte' (my dear marmot) (D8387), 'aimable marmotte' (kind marmot) (D10411), and 'suisse marmotte' (Swiss marmot) (D12168). Voltaire, it has to be said, is the more inventive: he signs off letters to Choiseul variously as 'la marmotte du mont Jura, ou le suisse V' (the marmot of Mt Jura, or the Swiss V' (D8864), 'la Marmotte des Alpes' (the marmot of the Alps) (D9147), and 'Agréez le profond respect de la marmotte. Voltaire' (Please accept the marmot's deepest respect. Voltaire (D10945). Voltaire can refer to himself as a third-person marmot in the body of a letter (D11887), and eventually the subscription of the marmot makes the final signature unnecessary, so that Voltaire can 'sign' a letter as 'Votre pauvre marmotte' (Your poor marmot) (D13975) or 'la vieille marmotte des alpes' (the old marmot of the Alps)

(D14906). The evocation of the marmot creates a special bond of intimacy between Voltaire and one particular correspondent; more than a signature, this image casts an intimacy over their whole correspondence. With other significant correspondents, Voltaire manages to build on the image to create an intimate network.

Voltaire as Pussycat

Beginning in January 1772, Voltaire, signing as 'Raton', writes to D'Alembert as 'Bertrand'. The allusion is to La Fontaine's fable 'Le singe et le chat', in which the cunning monkey Bertrand lets the cat Raton burn his paws extracting the chestnuts from the fire, only to eat them all himself. Voltaire and D'Alembert are firm allies in the Enlightenment crusade for reason against religious intolerance, and in the animal language of the fabulist, Voltaire poses as the gullible and obedient cat, burning his fingers as he performs useful work in the service of his manipulative and cunning friend. The image is, of course, flattering to D'Alembert, and their animal courtship continues until Voltaire's death six years later: in this wonderful literary extravaganza, Raton and Bertrand figure in no fewer than eighty-seven letters (Dawson, 1994). So Voltaire signs letters to D'Alembert as 'Le vieux Raton' (Old Raton) (D18485) or as 'Le vieux malingre Raton' (The old sickly Raton) (D18634); and in playing the part of La Fontaine's cat for so long, Voltaire creates, just once, what is perhaps the most plangent of all his 586 signatures: 'Miaou' (D18683).

There is a useful side to this practice. Voltaire is not alone in leaving letters to his friends unsigned, and rather surprisingly, this is sometimes a source of confusion for Voltaire himself. In a letter to D'Alembert of 1772 (D18118), Voltaire complains that '[Condorcet] ne signe point, et je prends quelquefois son écriture pour une autre. Cette méprise même m'est arrivée avec vous, mon cher philosophe' (Condorcet does not sign, and sometimes I take his handwriting for someone else's. This confusion has even happened with you, dear *philosophe*). So he suggests that they should sign with the first letter of their names or with some other 'monogram', concluding: 'Par exemple, je signe Raton, et Raton aime Bertrand de tout son cœur' (For example, I sign Raton, and Raton loves Bertrand with all his heart).

Beyond this practical use of the animal mask, it is a powerful source of literary creativity. As with the marmot impersonation, this is a game played in both directions and one that fully involves Voltaire's correspondent, thus creating a special bond between them. What makes this literary performance unique is that the use of the persona transcends the simple signature, so that the image of the monkey and the cat becomes integrated into their philosophical and political discussions. When Voltaire sends his books to his friend, he describes them as chestnuts: 'Mon cher philosophe aussi intrépide que circonspect, et qui avez grande raison d'être l'un et l'autre, voici une petite assiette de marrons que Raton envoie à son Bernard' (My dear philosopher, as intrepid as he is circumspect, and who has good reason to be both, here is a small plate of chestnuts that Raton sends his Bernard) (D18634). In a discussion of politics and superstition, Voltaire alludes to the difficulty of handling such a tricky subject: 'Voilà les marrons que Bertrand voit sous la cendre, et qui lui paroissent très bons à croquer; mais il a la patte trop lourde pour les tirer délicatement; vous voyez bien qu'il est nécessaire que Raton vienne au secours de Bertrand ' (These are the chestnuts that Bertrand can see beneath the ash, and that he thinks would be good to eat; but his paw is too clumsy to pull them out skilfully; you can see that it is necessary for Raton to come to Bertrand's aid) (D18145).

Then, from 1774, the young Condorcet enters the scene as a firm ally of D'Alembert, and Voltaire writes to them both as Bertrand, in the plural, opening a letter with 'Raton à messieurs Bertrands' (D19409). Voltaire, now over eighty years of age, is comforted by the presence and help of younger disciples, and the La Fontaine image is adapted to the new situation, as when he signs off one letter 'Raton met ses vieilles petites pattes entre les mains habiles des deux Bertrands; il remet tout à leur généreuse amitié' (Raton places his little old paws in the clever hands of the two Bertrands; he gives over everything to their generous friendship) (D19194). Another letter opens: 'Le vieux Raton se cache dans son coin derrière les Bertrands. Il leur écrit à tout deux, et voicy ce qu'il leur mande en miaulant' (Old Raton hides in his corner behind the Bertrands. He writes to them both, and here is what he meows to them) (D19653).

La Fontaine's fable becomes a form of philosophical shorthand at the same time as it enables real intimacy, as in this letter of 1774, written to a mutual friend, La Harpe – did La Harpe understand the potency of the references to Raton and Bernard?

> Il y a longtemps que je n'ai reçu de nouvelles de M^r D'Alembert, et que je ne lui ai écrit. La vieillesse et les maladies me rendent bien paresseux. Je vous prie, quand vous le verrez, de lui dire que Raton aimera Bertrand jusqu'au dernier soupir. Ce que je dis là pour lui je le dis pour vous.' (D18784)

> It has been a long time since I received any news from M. D'Alembert, and since I wrote to him. Old age and illnesses make me very lazy. I beg you, when you see him, to tell him that Raton will love Bertrand until his last breath. What I say for him, I say for you.

And here is D'Alembert, signing off a letter to Voltaire in January 1778 – it was the last letter he would ever send him (though they would meet in person):

'Adieu, mon cher et illustre maitre. Votre Bertrand embrasse bien tendrement les pattes de son cher et respectable Raton' (Farewell, my dear and illustrious master. Your Bertrand most tenderly kisses the paws of his dear and respectable Raton) (D21003). The two men, friends and allies over many decades, never achieved greater intimacy in their exchanges than when they were role-playing La Fontaine's cat and monkey.

2.4 Final Thoughts

Voltaire

Voltaire's signatures run the gamut of the alphabet: there are several letters signed 'A.' (for Arouet) and thousands signed 'V.' There is a 'Z' too. The first known letter (D1), written to his cousin in December 1704, when the young François-Marie was ten years old, is signed 'Zozo Arouet': the letter may be a forgery, which would be a shame, as if it is authentic, we can say that Voltaire runs the gamut from Z to A in his very first letter. His inventiveness in creating signatures for his letters is a key part of the self-invention that is central to the correspondence. Voltaire even invents a new art of not signing his letters by playing with the subscription. Signing off a letter to the actress Mlle Clairon, he produces a subscription containing not one but two neologisms: 'Ne comptez pas moins sur l'admiration et le tendre attachement du claironien et Antifréronien. V.' (Nevertheless you can count on the admiration and tender attachment of the Claironian and anti-Fréronian, V.) (D9240).[16] Some names in signatures are used just once, like 'Girafou' (D15858) or 'Martineau' (D15779); others, as we have seen, are used recurrently to create structures within the correspondence. Above all, Voltaire is endlessly playful, forever taking his reader by surprise. Except in formal letters, where convention is the necessary norm, he likes to keep his readers on their toes, and his letters characteristically have a sting in their tail. To doctor Tronchin, he signs off an enquiry about his niece's health as 'Trissotin Gengis Kan' (D9286): Trissotin, the pretentious pedant in Molière's comedy *Les Femmes savantes* is here yoked to Gengis-Kan, the brave hero of Voltaire's tragedy, *L'Orphelin de la Chine*,[17] and this burlesque amalgam of the pedantic warrior is a unique piece of self-representation designed specifically for the amusement of Tronchin. This is all a far cry from Denis Diderot, who signs a letter to Voltaire: 'Je suis &c. D.D.' (I am etc. D.D.) (D9430).

The fact remains that to recreate oneself 586 times is not just ludic: it is an ideological act. In Catholic teaching, baptism ranks first among the seven holy

---

[16] On Voltaire the neologist, see Section 3.
[17] On Voltaire's use and reuse of classical French literature, see Section 4.

sacraments, as the door through which the believer enters the Church; in baptism, a sacrament instituted by Christ, we are freed from the slavery of sin and reborn as sons of God. Voltaire demystifies the sacrament of baptism early in his *Lettres philosophiques* (1734). And perhaps his resolve to jettison his baptismal name, and his determined efforts perpetually to re-baptise himself are part of a broader project to demystify the Christian sacraments and the world at large. The act of baptising himself 586 times is one of joyous and glorious impiety.

Digital Editing

What can this necessarily limited investigation tell us about the promise and pitfalls of future digital collections, modelled, for the most part, after traditional critical editions such as those used by *EE*? In the spirit of this 'mixed mode' of traditional and digital criticism, we relied on the automatic extraction of subscriptions and signatures from the digital version of Voltaire's *Correspondence* found in the *EE* corpus; these results were then interpreted and contextualised using those time-honoured techniques of close reading generally associated with the print edition. This interplay of digital and traditional approaches is analogous, in many ways, to the interdisciplinary nature of the digital humanities, tasked with combining the often-segregated worlds of quantitative analysis and qualitative interpretation. Large-scale text databases like *EE* can move us in the direction of bridging the epistemological gap between the quantitative and the qualitative, provided that scholars are prepared to engage with these new technologies. At the same time, ever-expanding digital resources must also play their part in ensuring that the virtual availability (or 'searchability') of these texts still offers a meaningful level of deep interaction, and even some serendipity, when it comes to consulting online collections. To put it another way, the next generation of scholarly digital editions should strive to successfully mediate the competing strategies of 'distant' versus 'close' reading.

   With reference to our own study, the sort of 'value-added' document tagging that allowed us to consider all of Voltaire's signatures – an encoding scheme used increasingly by curated digital text collections such as *EE* – demonstrates precisely why traditional textual scholars should be more involved with the conception and production of digital editions. Indeed, the relatively simple data extraction and analysis that we used on the *EE* corpus would have been impossible with commercial online editions such as those offered by Google Books, or even HathiTrust, as they contain little to no structural encoding and often rely on un-corrected OCR (optical character recognition) to establish their texts. These resources, while to be applauded for their wide availability, leave much to be desired for scholarly purposes. It is precisely by way of the sort of 'value-added' digitisation efforts discussed here that current (and future) scholarly digital editions should strive not simply to mirror their 'analogue' forebears – those tried-and-true print critical editions – but instead attempt to reconceptualise the notion of textual scholarship in an increasingly digital and interconnected age. *EE* is one such attempt, and it is our hope that many more will be forthcoming. For our part, this modest exploration of Voltaire's signatures can be seen on some level as a rudimentary example of just how digital collections can change the scope and breadth of traditional scholarly enquiry.

3 Neologisms

3.1 Introduction

On matters of language, as on other topics, Voltaire holds strikingly contradictory ideas. On the one hand, he is culturally conservative and firmly supports the view that the French language had reached its peak of expressive perfection in the seventeenth century. This was an opinion shared by the majority of his contemporaries, who by and large considered French literary expression as 'fixed': any deviance from that standard could only be seen as the mark of decline (Brunot, 1932, pp. 863–72). Voltaire's *Siècle de Louis XIV* (*The Century of Louis XIV*), his widely read history of the reign of the Sun King, makes the point explicitly: 'Les grands hommes du siècle passé ont enseigné à penser et à parler' (The great men of the previous century taught [us] to think and to speak) (Voltaire, 1968–2021, vol. 13D, p. 25).

The grammarian Beauzée, writing in the *Encyclopédie* (specifically the articles 'Néologue' and 'Néologique'), adheres strictly to the orthodox position that new linguistic forms amount to linguistic corruption: 'Un auteur qui connoît les droits & les décisions de l'usage ne se sert que des mots reçus, ou ne se résout à en introduire de nouveaux que quand il y est forcé par une disette absolue & un besoin indispensable' (An author familiar with the rules and judgments of proper usage only uses received words, or only resolves to introduce new ones when he is forced to do so by an absolute scarcity and indispensable need) (Diderot, 1765, p. 94). Likewise, in his commentaries on the plays of Corneille, *Commentaires sur Corneille* (1764), Voltaire is unrelentingly critical of the linguistic 'faults' of the great tragedian (Voltaire, 1968–2021, vol. 54). This prejudice against lexical innovation is perhaps another vestige of Voltaire's Jesuit education, as one of his own teachers, the abbé d'Olivet, would become a leading opponent of neologism in the first half of the eighteenth century. Indeed, Olivet's *discours de réception* (maiden address) at the French Academy in 1723 can be read as a veritable manifesto for the cause of linguistic conservatism.[18]

Over the course of the eighteenth century, however, this view came increasingly to be challenged and, already in 1742, the poet Moncrif gives an address to the effect that one cannot and should not attempt to fix a living language: 'Qu'on ne peut ni ne doit fixer une langue vivante' (1751). By mid-century, the writer Marivaux had become notorious for coining new words to express, so he argued, new nuances of emotion. His critics dismissed this 'marivaudage' as a new form of seventeenth-century preciosity, and Voltaire was predictably scathing about this breach of classical linguistic etiquette. Yet gradually more and more writers claimed the right to create neologisms as a matter of creative liberty, and for the *philosophes* in particular, there was an understanding that the language might need to evolve to take account of new ways of thinking (Seguin, 1972; Mervaud, 2011). As the party of the *philosophes* became increasing dominant in the French Academy from the 1760s on, so the Academy became increasingly open to the idea of those who, like Marmontel, held that neologism was perhaps a positive thing.

Even Voltaire rallied to this point of view. In 1778, close to death, at his last appearance at the Académie française he laid out his plan for a new dictionary, making the case for a restoration of the 'picturesque and energetic' terms of Renaissance writers like Amyot and Montaigne (Voltaire, 1968–2021, vol. 80 c, p. 421). More than twenty years later, in 1801, Louis Sébastien Mercier would publish his work *Néologie, ou vocabulaire de mots nouveaux*.[19] Mercier was far from being an unconditional admirer of Voltaire, and yet it is Voltaire who is here the most frequently cited source of neologisms. He is hugely prominent in this book, and the title page even has an epigraph drawn from Voltaire's correspondence: 'Notre langue est une gueuse fière; il faut lui faire l'aumône malgré elle' (our language is a proud beggar; we need to give her alms despite herself) (a misquotation of a letter to Frederick II, D4001).

Attentive readers of Voltaire have always appreciated his linguistic inventiveness, a key part of his stylistic playfulness, which seems to be in contradiction with his avowed conservatism in matters of language. This is especially apparent in his correspondence, where we often have the sense that Voltaire can 'let his hair down' (remove his wig?) and experiment with a freer form of expression. We might go so far as to venture the hypothesis that Voltaire uses the correspondence as a sort of linguistic laboratory to try out his lexical inventions before employing them in the wider public sphere. To test this hypothesis one

---

[18] See www.academie-francaise.fr/discours-de-reception-de-labbe-dolivet.
[19] See the excellent critical edition by Jean-Claude Bonnet (2009).

was, until recently, reliant on the intuitions of the close reader and the identification of largely anecdotal evidence. In this section we are addressing the question head-on: how can we describe Voltaire's recourse to neologism in his letters more precisely than before and from a more distant perspective?

3.2 The Experiment

The task of identifying neologisms in any corpus, much less one the size of Voltaire's, is decidedly non-trivial.[20] Luckily, however, we can now bank on the past two centuries of lexicographic research and the growing availability of online dictionary resources in French. Thanks to previous work at the University of Chicago's ARTFL Project compiling and developing the *Dictionnaire vivant de la langue française* (Allen et al., 2011), whose interface federates searches across ten French-language dictionaries,[21] we were able to access machine-readable versions of Émile Littré's nineteenth-century *Dictionnaire de la langue française* (4 vols., 1873–7) as well as the more recent and comprehensive *Trésor de la langue française informatisé* (11 vols., 1971– 94).[22] Using the structured data that underlie these digital resources, again in the form of XML-encoded files, we were able to query the multiple citations of Voltaire presented as lexical use-cases in these dictionaries and, eventually, to identify examples of first-uses, or neologisms.

In the first instance, the Littré dictionary proved both overwhelmingly rich in Voltaire citations – including a great many drawn from his letters – and, at the same time, relatively poor in terms of the information needed to identify Voltaire's neologisms systematically. The Littré is riddled with literary citations – some 297,000 in fact – that are used to elucidate lexical definitions. Voltaire is by far the most cited author for Littré, with 18,023 citations drawn from his works, compared to Bossuet's 12,000 and roughly 11,000 each for Corneille and Racine. As a whole, the correspondence is mined for use-cases some 4,129 times – making it one of the most cited literary 'works' in the entire dictionary, just behind Montaigne's *Essais* and Amyot's *Vies des hommes illustres* (itself a translation of Plutarch). Voltaire's letters are thus, by Littré's time, established as a literary monument, cited three times as often as either his *Dictionnaire philosophique* (1,430 citations) or the *Essai sur les mœurs* (1,382 citations), although quotations from letters are at times incomplete or at odds with modern editions – a reflection of how the correspondence as a corpus of

---

[20] For recent work using machine learning and French newspapers, see Falk et al., 2014.

[21] https://dvlf.uchicago.edu/.

[22] Data for these dictionaries were made available by the XMLittré project (www.littre.org) and the Centre national de ressources textuelles et lexicales CNRTL (www.cnrtl.fr) respectively.

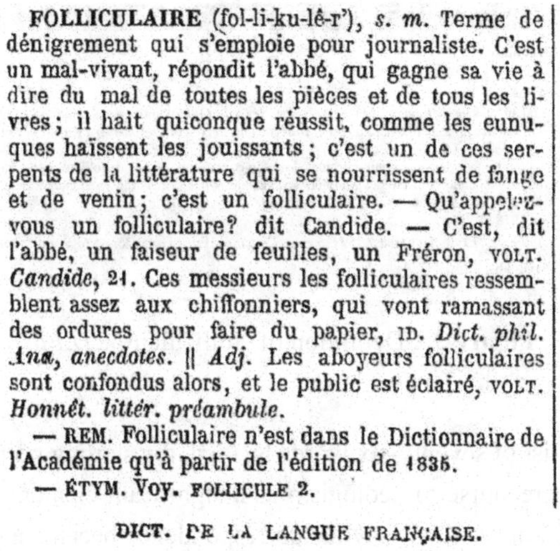

FOLLICULAIRE (fol-li-ku-lê-r'), *s. m.* Terme de dénigrement qui s'emploie pour journaliste. C'est un mal-vivant, répondit l'abbé, qui gagne sa vie à dire du mal de toutes les pièces et de tous les livres; il hait quiconque réussit, comme les eunuques haïssent les jouissants; c'est un de ces serpents de la littérature qui se nourrissent de fange et de venin; c'est un folliculaire. — Qu'appelez-vous un folliculaire? dit Candide. — C'est, dit l'abbé, un faiseur de feuilles, un Fréron, VOLT. *Candide*, 21. Ces messieurs les folliculaires ressemblent assez aux chiffonniers, qui vont ramassant des ordures pour faire du papier, ID. *Dict. phil. Ana, anecdotes.* ‖ *Adj.* Les aboyeurs folliculaires sont confondus alors, et le public est éclairé, VOLT. *Honnêt. littér. préambule.*
— REM. Folliculaire n'est pas dans le Dictionnaire de l'Académie qu'à partir de l'édition de 1835.
— ÉTYM. Voy. FOLLICULE 2.

DICT. DE LA LANGUE FRANÇAISE.

Figure 3.1 Definition of 'folliculaire', Littré, Dictionnaire de la langue française

letters was, and is, in a constant state of flux, growing and changing with each subsequent edition.

The structure of the Littré, both in print and online, makes it difficult, if not impossible, however, to identify automatically citations that attest to first usages, either in Voltaire or any other source. To take Voltaire's most famous neologism, 'folliculaire' (a pejorative moniker for a Grub Street journalist – a 'rag-monger'?): the term was coined, as we shall see, while writing *Candide*, but Littré's incorporation of use-cases with the definitions (see Fig. 3.1) makes it difficult to distinguish first-uses from *exempla*, thus leaving one to guess as to whether first attestations from Voltaire are meant to represent neologisms or are simply useful demonstrations of a particular word-use. For our purposes, then, the more explicit structure of the *TLF* and, in particular, its online version, the *TLFi*, which effectively expands and builds upon the Littré knowledge base, offered us more discernible data, making first-uses identifiable.

The definition for 'folliculaire' in the *TLFi*, along with new examples from more modern authors – Chateaubriand, Murger, and Proust – has a separate rubric for etymology and history, wherein the first attestation of usage is given with a date, in this case Voltaire's 1759 use in *Candide* (see Fig. 3.2). Using the structured data of the *TLFi*, we were thus able to extract all instances in which 'Voltaire' is mentioned in the 'Étymol. et Hist.' section across the 270,000 definitions included in the *TLFi*. From these, we generated a list of sixty-five words for which Voltaire is given as the first attestation, and of an additional eleven words that appear early in Voltaire but for which first-use is difficult to

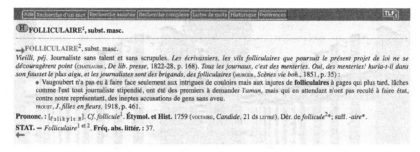

Figure 3.2 Definition of 'folliculaire', *TLFi*

ascertain. This list of seventy-six words is, then, the starting point for thinking about Voltaire's recourse to neologism as a significant element of his writing style, and more importantly, how his correspondence became a catalyst in the coining of new terms.

These attestations drawn from the *TLFi*, however, by no means tell the whole story of Voltaire's lexicon: first, as the *TLFi* was compiled in the 1970s and finished in 1994, modern databases of Voltaire's complete works and correspondence were not yet available to its editors; second, even though Besterman's edition of the correspondence was well under way in the 1970s, it is likely that lexicographers at the *TLF*, like Émile Littré before them, relied on nineteenth-century editions of Voltaire's letters, which were far from comprehensive. To put it bluntly, no matter how high the quality of research that went into these dictionaries, they were reliant largely on incomplete editions of Voltaire's works and letters.

In establishing the Voltaire Lab, one of our first goals was to constitute a research database that brings together all of Voltaire's writings and the most up-to-date version of his correspondence drawn from *EE*. Expanding on the publicly available *TOUT Voltaire* database, we christened the new database *TV2*, a resource that makes search and exploration across the entirety of Voltaire's written output – works and letters together – possible for the first time. *TV2* proved incredibly helpful in analysing Voltaire's creation, use, and reuse of neologisms. For the following analysis, we located the first instance of word-use in the *TV2* database for each of our seventy-six possible neologisms and compared these with similar searches in the ARTFL-Frantext database, which allowed us to catch earlier usages which might previously have gone unnoticed and, at the same time, track the later history of Voltaire's neologisms in the wider world of French letters.

3.3 Analysis

Using the above method, we established a list of thirty neologisms that Voltaire uses first in his correspondence (see Table 3.1):

Table 3.1 Neologisms that first occur in Voltaire's correspondence

Neologism	Letter
abrutisseur	D15868, to D'Alembert, 1769
alentours	D13278, to the marquis de Florian, 1766
anecdotier	D1137, to Henri Pitot, 1736
aplatisseur	D2526, to Maupertuis, 1741
arrière-cousin	D5011, to d'Argental, 1752
athéistique	D15189, to the marquis de Villevieille, 1768
attorney	D15140, to Horace Walpole, 1768
autocratrice	D1935, to Antioch Cantemir, 1739
commodore	D9325, to Jean Robert Tronchin, 1760
coucherie	D9244, to comte and comtesse d'Argental, 1760
fumiste	D897, to de Roncières, 1735
grianneau	D7188, to the marquise de Florian, 1757
gribouillage	D2540, to Maupertuis, 1741
inélastique	D24252, to Dortous de Mairan, 1741
injouable	D995, to Thiriot, 1736
inoculable	D7711, to Mme D'Épinay, 1758
invendable	D5554, to the comtesse de Lutzelbourg, 1753
jérémiade	D253, to Thiriot, 1725
jouable	D2408, to the comte d'Argental, 1741
nasillonneur	D16841, to D'Alembert, 1770
ostensible	D1735, to Thiriot, 1739
patriarchal	D6214, to the comtesse de Lutzelbourg, 1755
rabâchage	D870, to Thiriot, 1735
rabâcheur	D10323, to D'Alembert, 1762
racinien	D11253, to Gabriel Cramer, 1763
retranscrire	D2430, to the comte d'Argental, 1741
shakespearien	D20986, to La Harpe, 1778
tolérantisme	D391, to Jean François Du Bellay, 1730
triplicate	D7724, to Jean Robert Tronchin, 1758
versiculet	D536, to Cideville, 1732

Of course, the definition of a neologism is not and cannot be absolutely precise. What are we to make, for example, of the word *attorney*, first used by Voltaire in 1768, when he writes flatteringly to Horace Walpole, 'Vous seriez un excellent attorney general; vous pesez toutes les probabilités' (D15140): is this a borrowing from English amounting to a creation in the French language, or simply the quotation of an English word to an English correspondent? In other cases, Voltaire may not be the first to coin a word, although he may be the first to establish it definitively in the French language: it seems that Jacques Cazotte first uses the word *alentours* in 1763, though Voltaire's use in a letter of 1766 is quite possibly independent of Cazotte's usage.

Ostensible is used to describe a letter designed to be shown to a third party. It is an interesting word in this context, as it describes a key aspect of Voltaire's epistolary practice, for example, when he writes to the printer of one of his potentially dangerous works, denying his authorship: of course, the printer will not believe a word of it, but the letter is useful for the printer to have in case the police pay him a visit. According to the Frantext database, the word is first used in this sense by Saint-Simon in 1691, but it does not seem to have caught on at that stage, and it is hard not to think that it is Voltaire who gives the term its currency. Voltaire first uses the word in a letter to Thiriot in January 1739 (D1735), and it recurs thereafter in some 100 letters. In fact, *EE* reveals that Voltaire's companion Émilie Du Châtelet uses the word in a letter to d'Argental a few weeks before Voltaire's first known usage, on 29 December 1738 (D1723): it rather looks as if the couple must have been using the word between themselves as they discussed epistolary strategy. Certainly, the mark of a successful word is that it is used in return by friends, as when D'Alembert uses the term, underlined, in a letter to Voltaire in 1768 (D14922).

Émilie Du Châtelet is clearly an interesting neologist in her own right. The word *rabâcheur*, used to describe someone who endlessly repeats the same material, is one that Voltaire uses often, for example in a letter to D'Alembert in 1762 (D10323); D'Alembert uses the word back to him in a letter later the same year (D10805). Voltaire is almost certainly the writer who puts this word into general circulation, though Frantext again attests to an earlier usage in Rousseau's *Lettre à D'Alembert* (1758). In fact, *EE* shows us that the first use of all seems to be by Du Châtelet, in a letter to Frederick II in 1740: 'Mais je ne sais si votre altesse royale a lu un rabâcheur français qu'on appelle Montaigne' (D2202). It is entirely possible that Voltaire learned the word – along with a great many other things – first from Emilie Du Châtelet.[23]

But even with these caveats, and taking into account the unavoidable imprecisions involved with this type of investigation, this list of neologisms remains impressive. Voltaire's linguistic creativity covers a wide chronological span, from *jérémiade* (1725) to *shakespearien* (1778) in the last year of his life. There is creative energy in a word like *abrutisseur*, describing to D'Alembert the brutalising influence of the Turks: 'Les affaires des Turcs vont mal. Je voudrais bien que ces marauds là fussent chassés du pays de Périclès et de Platon: il est

---

[23] The most recent version of the *TLFi* now includes this first usage by Du Châtelet in 1740, replacing Littré's attribution to the later letters between Voltaire and D'Alembert.

vrai qu'ils ne sont pas persécuteurs, mais ils sont *abrutisseurs*. Dieu nous défasse des uns et des autres!' (The Turks' affairs are going badly. I would like these rascals to be chased out of the land of Pericles and Plato: it is true that they are not persecutors, but they are *brutalisers*. May God free us of both!) (D15868). And Voltaire has an uncanny ability to leave his mark on certain words: he not only coins *versiculet* in 1732, a self-deprecating way of referring to his occasional verses as 'mes petits versiculets', but he uses the term over and over again in letters to close friends, Cideville, Thiriot, Marie-Louise Denis, the duc de Richelieu, the d'Argentals, Boufflers, the marquis de Villette, Damiliaville, the marquise Du Deffand, and so on – Voltaire, famous as a master of occasional verse, imposes this word on those most important to him.

We note how the words to some extent group into thematic areas of particular relevance to Voltaire. The largest thematic group is concerned with writing: *anecdotier* (anecdotist), *gribouillage* (scribbling), *jérémiade* (attack), *versiculet* (minor verse), *retranscrire* (retranscribe), *rabâchage* (repetition), *rabâcheur* (a churner-out of the same stuff), and *triplicate* (triplicate); *jouable* (performable) and *injouable* (unperformable) are to do with theatre; *ostensible* (showable) to do with letters; and not to be forgotten are the adjectives calqued on writers' names: *racinien* and *shakespearien*. Another cluster of terms is concerned with Voltaire's philosophical outlook: *athéistique* (atheistic), *tolérantisme* (toleration), *patriarchal* (patriarchal), and *inoculable* (inoculable) – and as a mark of Voltaire's influence, it is worth noting that *tolérantisme* is subsequently adopted by the abbé Raynal in his *Histoire philosophique des deux Indes* (1770). In keeping with Voltaire's satirical verve, some of the words are coined to describe a particular individual: *aplatisseur*, *autocratrice*, and *nasillonneur*. *Aplatisseur* (flattener) is the word he uses for Maupertuis, who proved that the Earth was flattened at the poles. *Nasillonneur* (a speaker through the nose) is coined to describe pejoratively the président de Brosses, with whom he was embroiled in a lawsuit: 'le président nasillonneur', 'petit persécuteur nasillonneur', 'ce fripon de nasillonneur', and so on (the nasalising president, the little nasalising persecutor, this nasalising rogue) become common currency in letters to his friends who shared his view of the man.

Epistolary manuals of the period taught that the style of a letter should imitate good conversation, and in keeping with this principle several of these neologisms have a familiar, even pejorative, flavour: in addition to words already cited (*nasillonneur, rabâchage, rabâcheur, anecdotier, gribouillage*), there are also *abrutisseur* and *coucherie*. When Voltaire coins the word *coucherie* to describe sexual activity, it is in the context of a humorous letter designed to please the comte and comtesse d'Argental: 'Il y a beaucoup de coucherie, mais c'est en tout bien et en tout honneur' (There's plenty of sex, but it's all in a good cause) (D9244). And, as mentioned above, it is a mark of success when a neologism is used back to the coiner: D'Alembert uses the term in writing to Voltaire, where it figures in a list of Enlightenment freedoms: 'si la presse, la religion, et la *coucherie* sont également libres en France [. . .]' (if the press, religion, and sex are equally free in France . . .) (D11541). Voltaire's coinages in his letters often have a personal as well as a jokey flavour: *inoculable*, meaning someone who undergoes inoculation, has an obvious philosophical ring (Voltaire had advocated the practice), but he coins this term in writing to Louise d'Épinay, who had made a point of inoculating her young son. So Voltaire coins the word referring to her son as 'l'inoculable' (D7711), then the following year refers to her as 'Ma belle inoculable, ma courageuse philosophe' (My inoculable beauty, my courageous philosopher) (D8419).

Not surprisingly, many of these neologisms pass later into his other writings: *arrière-cousin* and *tolérantisme* both reappear in the *Essai sur les mœurs* (1756); *autocratrice*, used widely in the correspondence before appearing in the *Commentaire sur le livre Des délits et des peines* (1766); *grianneau*, a rare term for a bird that later occurs in the *Lettre de M. Clocpicre à M. Eratou* (1761); *invendable* and *patriarchal* both reappear in the *Questions sur l'Encyclopédie* (1770–2); and *jérémiade* is later used in the play *L'Enfant prodigue* (1736).

It is also interesting to consider the neologisms that are first used in Voltaire's writings other than the letters. Table 3.2 shows the thirty-six words first used in his works, along with the work in question – the neologisms that are later reused in the letters are marked with an asterisk.

When, during the election campaign of 2017, Emmanuel Macron declared his wish to be 'un président jupitérien', he possibly did not know he was giving new life to a Voltairean neologism. Neither of these lists is meant to be definitive. There are other neologisms, like *marginer* and *réfracter*, that appear more or less simultaneously in the letters and the works. *Cuissage* is in fact an archaic term that Voltaire, for obviously humorous reasons, brings back into circulation. And there are other terms that Voltaire uses soon after the first attested use and that he may well have helped to put into circulation, including *aberration*, *antipoétique*, *arlequinade*, *autodafé*, *baladinage*, *biribi*, *croquis*, *décloîtrer*, *triquer*, and *vulgivague*.

3.4 Final Thoughts

Our experiment tends to confirm the intuition of Louis-Sébastien Mercier that Voltaire – although he publicly professed otherwise – was perhaps the most prominent neologist of his age. The lists of Voltaire's neologisms produced here are nonetheless very different from Mercier's list, which contains many terms

Table 3.2 Neologisms that appear first in Voltaire's works

Neologism	Work
agoniste	*Dictionnaire philosophique*, 1764
aï (vin d')	*Le Mondain*, 1736
antipatriotique	*L'Homme aux quarante écus*, 1768
barcarolle*	*Sémiramis*, 1746
bernable*	*L'Enfant prodigue*, 1736
cavagnol(e)*	*Les Originaux ou M. du Cap-Vert*, 1738
cuissage*	*Essai sur les mœurs*, 1756
décasquer	*La Pucelle d'Orléans*, 1755
définisseur*	*Questions sur l'Encyclopédie*, 1770–2
folliculaire*	*Candide*, 1759
giton*	*L'Anti-Giton*, 1714
incohérent*	*Les Pourquoi*, 1742
indébrouillable	*Dictionnaire philosophique*, 1764
insocial*	*Histoire de l'empire de Russie*, 1759
indécomposable	*Éléments de la philosophie de Newton*, 1736
indéfinissable	*Lettres philosophiques*, 1734
irrévérencieux*	*La Bible enfin expliquée*, 1776
joaniste*	*Examen important de milord Bolingbroke*, 1766
jupitérien*	*Les Pourquoi*, 1742
leibnizien*	*Éléments de la philosophie de Newton*, 1736
logos*	*Essai sur les mœurs*, 1756
loquace	*Il faut prendre un parti*, 1772
milady*	*To milady Hervey*, 1726
meeting	*Questions sur l'Encyclopédie*, 1770–2
omniscience	*Traité de métaphysique*, 1734
perfectible	*Essai sur les mœurs*, 1756
prélibation	*Essai sur les mœurs*, 1756
protectorat	*Le Siècle de Louis XIV*, 1751
quadrisaïeul	*Précis du siècle de Louis XV*, 1745
scandinave	*Annales de l'Empire*, 1753
show	*Les Lois de Minos*, 1771
sténographie	*Questions sur l'Encyclopédie*, 1770–2
superstructure	*Commentaires sur Corneille*, 1761
tyrolien	*Candide*, 1759
ukrainien	*Histoire de Charles XII*, 1727
Zend*	*Zadig*, 1747

Words marked with an asterisk reoccur in the correspondence.

no longer in frequent usage and that have thus fallen out of modern dictionaries like the *TLFi*. Likewise, the above work also confirms our long-standing personal intuition that the ability to cross-reference digital resources – from dictionaries to databases – can be a boon to lexicographers and literary scholars alike.

We have found a number of cases where searches in *EE* can improve on the information found in all the standard reference dictionaries: this is perhaps an example of the dynamism of correspondences in general and their role in helping to generate new linguistic usages. For example, Littré cites as the first usage of *injouable* (unperformable) a letter of Voltaire's from 1767 (D13787); *EE* leads us to two earlier usages in the Voltaire correspondence: D995 (1736) and D8350 (1759). Sometimes *EE* helps us not only to find an earlier usage but also to change the identity of the neologist. Both Littré and the *TLF* say that the first usage of *terraqué* is in Voltaire's *Memnon*; but *EE* shows us that the term was already used by Jean-Jacques Rousseau in a letter to the *Mercure de France*, dated 1738. Littré gives the first usage of *aplatisseur* as being in a letter from Voltaire to Maupertuis, dated 6 October 1741 (D2550). *EE* shows us a slightly earlier occurrence, also in a letter from Voltaire to Maupertuis (D2526, 10 August 1741). But that is not the end of the story: in fact, it was apparently Frederick II who first coined the jokey term, in a letter to Voltaire dated 14 May 1741: 'Vous ignorez que Maupertuis, cet aplatisseur de la terre ... ' (You are unaware that Maupertuis, that flattener of the earth ...) (D2481).

Digital experiments are especially strong at identifying patterns of repetition and exchange, and beyond the specific evidence of first usage presented here, our research suggests that what is really interesting about neologisms is how they are often deeply embedded in social exchanges; this is arguably more important than simply identifying an isolated individual as first user of a given word. At the same time, one cannot fail to be struck by the energy of Voltaire's linguistic inventions, ensuring that he has exercised a lasting influence on the French language. The word *bernable*, 'capable of being tricked', seems harmless enough – Voltaire first coins it in his comedy *L'Enfant prodigue* (1736); it was admitted by the Académie in 1762. But precisely how Voltaire uses the term, in a letter to the comte d'Argental, is worth noting: 'Car je l'ai berné, car je suis berneur, car il est bernable' (for I've tricked him, for I'm a trickster, for he is trickable) (D10147, 1761). This is a bravura use of a new word, as he improvises on the verb *berner* to produce two unfamiliar but entirely comprehensible terms based on the same stem. Voltaire can make poetry with neologism.

Perhaps one of the most famous neologisms, already mentioned, is *folliculaire*, used pejoratively in *Candide* to describe a Grub Street journalist, coined at a time when the *philosophes* generally were the subject of vicious attack in the press and elsewhere. *Candide* appeared in early 1759, and at about the same time, on 5 January, Voltaire uses the term in a letter to the Protestant pastor Élie Bertrand (D8029): it is hard to say here which of the two has priority, and the coining of this term shows the symbiosis that exists between Voltaire's works and his letter-writing. What is interesting here is that the new word *folliculaire* recurs some twenty-seven more times in the letters – so much so that from 1763 (D10978) onward, many of his correspondents, including Frederick II (D20954), take up the term and reuse it in writing back to him. Clearly, Voltaire's linguistic creativity was widely recognised in his own lifetime, though the scope and scale of this inventiveness are only now beginning to emerge. Despite his apparent conservatism on questions of linguistic change, Voltaire has undeniably left a permanent mark on the French language.

4 Quotations | French

4.1 Introduction

In his story *Les Deux Consolés*, Voltaire features a philosopher called 'Citophile', 'lover of quotations' – a moniker that could as easily be applied to Voltaire himself. Quotation of the classics occupies a prominent place in early modern literary culture. 'Humanists typically viewed themselves as drawing on common sources of knowledge,' writes James Bednarz (2018, p. 44); 'And although Dryden called Jonson a "learned" plagiarist, there was never a consensus in the early modern period about how much of another's recognisable language and ideas one might use before being accused of being merely parasitic.' So quotation, even though encouraged and expected, nonetheless had to be handled with care. Voltaire's writing is profoundly enriched by the literature he had memorised, in part a result of his Jesuit schooling, as we shall see in Section 5. He is, moreover, in permanent and dynamic dialogue with the authors he reads, as evidenced by the books in his library, lavishly covered with his marginal comments, some of which consist of quotations from one author penned in the margins of another (Pink, 2018, pp. 63–66).

The letters are no exception in their widespread use of literary quotation. This phenomenon has been studied only to a very limited extent: François Bessire (1999) has examined the place of the Bible in the correspondence, and Daniel Calvez (1989) has also studied the use of proverbs in the letters. Besterman himself provides an 'Index of quotations' (Voltaire, 1968–2021, vol. 135, col. 1029–92) that hints at the riches to be found in the letters, yet even this is not entirely satisfactory, as our investigation will show.

The challenge, then, is to see to what extent digital methods can supplement the existing work in this area and ideally uncover new terrain for exploration.

Biblical quotations are without doubt the most frequent and perhaps the easiest to understand – Biblical quotation was a trope with all writers of this period (Gibert, 2010). Latin texts are also present, and in Section 5 we examine Voltaire's quotations of Latin poets. Here, however, we shall focus exclusively on his numerous quotations from the French literary tradition.

4.2 The Experiment

It is possible to identify Voltaire's use and reuse of French quotations by comparing his letters with a corpus of French literary texts. Concretely, for this experiment we made use of the TextPAIR[24] sequence alignment algorithm developed by the ARTFL Project and designed to identify text reuse across datasets (Olsen et al., 2011; Roe, 2012). This particular technique has been used previously to uncover patterns of citation and non-citation in the *Encyclopédie* (Edelstein et al., 2012) as well as unacknowledged contributions to this same work by Émilie Du Châtelet (Roe, 2018). We thus compared Voltaire's letters to 1,133 works of French literature drawn from the ARTFL-Frantext database mentioned in Section 3.2 on neologisms. The works selected were all published before 1778, the year of Voltaire's death, while excluding Voltaire's own works and any other writer's correspondence from the comparison corpus. While the system identified more than 1,700 shared passages between Frantext and Voltaire's letters, many of these are repeated quotations of a single author or indeed false positive matches such as long formulaic phrases common to certain genres (e.g., epistolary novels). By filtering out this noise as much as possible, we were able to sketch a general outline of Voltaire's use of French literary quotations in his letters.

By far the largest block of quotations comes from authors of the seventeenth century, the so-called Classical period (see Table 4.1). The pre-Classical period is surprisingly under-represented in the correspondence, with only single passages taken from Jean Bertaut and Rabelais, though the passage quoted from the latter is used in six separate letters. Contemporary writers from the (long) eighteenth century are predictably more present, though by no means as prevalent as their Classical counterparts (see Table 4.2).

---

[24] https://github.com/ARTFL-Project/text-pair. Text-PAIR works by pre-processing texts into 'n-grams' (e.g., a group of *n* words occurring in sequence), with high-frequency function words filtered out. When a matching pair of n-grams (in our experiment we use trigrams, or groups of three words in sequence) is identified, the system then evaluates the succeeding n-grams to assess if the passages are in fact related. There are several parameters for more flexible matching evaluation, such as how many n-grams can be skipped over, which allows us to find similar though not identical passages between two databases.

Table 4.1 Seventeenth-century authors quoted by Voltaire in his letters

Author	Number of quotations
Racine	38
Boileau	36
Corneille	33
La Fontaine	27
Molière	20
Quinault	7
Fontenelle	2
La Rochefoucauld	1

Table 4.2 Eighteenth-century authors quoted by Voltaire in his letters

Author	Number of quotations
Jean-Jacques Rousseau	4
Marmontel	3
Saint-Lambert	3
Jean-Baptiste Rousseau	3
Crébillon père	2
Helvétius	2
D'Alembert	1
d'Argenson	1
La Noue	1
Duclos	1
Nivelle de La Chaussée	1

4.3 Defining a Quotation

Clearly, these tables cannot be treated with absolute precision. Some quotations have inevitably been missed, and of course there is an important question concerning how exactly we define a quotation in the first place. Moreover, the tables list only instances where there is a citation of a work found in the correspondence; those cases where Voltaire mentions works simply by their title or author without giving significant extracts fall outside the category of text reuse.

In addition, the TextPAIR system finds 'related' passages – that is, exact or near-exact quotes with some flexibility – but is not built to find allusions. For example, Voltaire went to great lengths to plan the marriage of Marie-Françoise

Corneille (the great-niece of the dramatist), and at the last moment the plans collapsed because the groom's family refused to provide any dowry. Explaining this to the Président de Ruffey, Voltaire writes: 'Je vous dirai que celuy qui se proposait pour épouser Mlle Corneille était M. de Cormont, capitaine de cavalerie, fils du commissaire des guerres de Chalons. Je donnais une dot honnête, mais le commissaire ne donnait rien du tout; et la raison sans dot n'a pas réussi' (I can tell you that the man who was proposing to marry Mlle Corneille was M. de Cormont, a cavalry captain, son of the army commissioner of Chalons. I offered an honest dowry, but the commissioner offered nothing at all; and reason without dowry did not persuade) (D10910). This last phrase is a clear allusion to the famous scene in Molière's *L'Avare* (1.7) in which the miser Harpagon finds utterly persuasive the 'reason' of a groom who accepts a bride with no dowry – 'sans dot'. This allusion to one of Molière's most celebrated comic scenes (itself a quotation of a scene from a comedy by Plautus) would have been evident to Voltaire's correspondent, and of course adds humour to an explanation that Voltaire otherwise finds embarrassing to relate. But such an allusion is not a quotation and so for the time being falls outside our particular experiment.

Our list therefore does not pretend to comprehensiveness, but it contains much matter for thought. To begin with, when is a quotation not a quotation? Voltaire often signs off to friends with 'Vivez heureux' (Live happily) or 'Vivez longtemps' (Live long) – which, in itself, is hardly a quotation. But what about 'Vivez heureux, vivez longtemps, et conservez moi vos bontés' (Live happily, live long, and continue your kindness to me) (D11633) or, to the duc de Richelieu, 'Vivez heureux et vivez longtemps, voilà mon refrain. La nation a besoin de vous' (Live happily and live long, that is my refrain. The nation needs you) (D13502)? Neither of these last two examples is identified as a quotation by Besterman, but our results point us to a passage sung by the chorus in Corneille's machine tragedy *Andromède* (4.6):

> Vivez, vivez, heureux amants,
> Dans les douceurs que l'amour vous inspire;
> Vivez heureux, et vivez si longtemps,
> Qu'au bout d'un siècle entier on puisse encore vous dire:
> 'Vivez, heureux amants'

> Live, live, happy lovers / in the gentleness that love inspires; / Live happy
> Live, happy lovers / When a hundred years have passed, may you still be
> told: / 'Live, happy lovers'

It is hard to think Voltaire did not have this passage in mind, and there are other examples too: 'Vivez heureux et longtemps' (D9538), 'Adieu, vivez heureux et longtemps, mon cher maître' (to his former teacher, Pierre Joseph Thoulier d'Olivet, D13233), 'Vivez heureusement, gaiement, et longtemps' (D14667), and 'Vivez heureux tous deux très longtemps' (D16986).

A quotation can be proverbial, like Montaigne's 'Que sais-je?' (What do I know?) (*Essais*, 2.12), an expression of scepticism entirely in keeping with Voltaire's own philosophy. When he writes, 'Je suis ici depuis huit jours, mon cher philosophe, j'y passerai quelques mois, peut-être l'hiver, que sais-je? J'aurai donc le temps d'y recevoir de vos nouvelles' (I have been here for eight days, my dear *philosophe*, I shall stay a few months, perhaps for the winter, who knows? So I shall have the time to hear your news) (D20850), his use of the expression is a rhetorical tic and clearly not a quotation of Montaigne. However, when Voltaire writes to Frederick II in 1738 (D1506), 'vous prenez encore ce mot de Montaigne, *que sais-je?* pour votre devise' (you still take the Montaigne phrase, *what do I know?* as your motto), the quotation is clear. Thirty-two years later, in 1770, Frederick uses the same phrase in a letter to Voltaire: 'Après les belles lettres, dans l'âge de la réflexion, vient la philosophie; et quand nous l'avons bien étudiée, nous sommes obligés de dire comme Montaigne: Que sais je?' (After literature, in the age of reflexion, comes philosophy; and when we have studied it well, we are obliged to say, with Montaigne: What do I know?) (D16667). The Montaigne tag defines and encapsulates their philosophical exchanges of over thirty years.

Another quotation-cum-proverb is 'magis magnos clericos non sunt magis magnos sapientes' (the greatest clerks are not the wisest men), which is found in Rabelais's *Gargantua* (1534), and then prominently quoted by Montaigne in his *Essais* ('Du pédantisme', 1.25). The identification of this invented Latin proverb, from the pen of a French author no less, in effect prefigures Section 5 on Latin quotations. Voltaire, as we can tell from the correspondence, reread Rabelais in 1758 – just at the time that he was writing *Candide* – and he uses the quotation that year in a letter to D'Alembert (D7651). It was obviously pertinent to the quarrels and debates surrounding the *philosophes* at the time, and Voltaire uses it on five further occasions, to D'Alembert (D7842, D18473), Helvétius (D9069), Damilaville (D11353), and to an unknown recipient in 1773 (D18620). In these cases, the quotation was clearly familiar to his correspondents and it functions almost as a rallying cry for the *philosophes*.

Quotations of verse tend to stand out in prose, so are more easily identifiable, whereas a prose quotation or paraphrase is easily missed. A 1741 letter to 'sGravesande (D2519), for example, contains a clear, though not identical, reference to Pascal's *De l'esprit géometrique*:

> 'Toutes les fois qu'une proposition est inconcevable il ne faut pas la nier mais examiner le contraire, et s'il est manifestement faux on peut affirmer le contraire tout incompréhensible qu'il est'.[25]

> Every time a proposition is inconceivable, one should not deny it but examine the contrary, and if it is manifestly false, one can affirm the contrary, however incomprehensible.

Voltaire's relation to Pascal is important and notoriously complex – in this case, it seems we have identified a significant source that was until now hidden in plain sight.

4.4 Quoting Classics from the Age of the Sun King

Given what we know about Voltaire's predilection for authors from the age of Louis XIV, it is not surprising that French classical authors are widely quoted (see Table 4.3).

The below numbers are merely indicative, as some passages reoccur in different letters. Of the works of Jean Racine, the most quoted author, it is his comedy, *Les Plaideurs*, that comes top with eight quotes. This is partly because one quotation, 'Ma foi, juge et plaideurs, il faudroit tout' (My goodness, judge and litigants, we need everything) (1.8) is used four times. This line, uttered by the porter Petit Jean, brings down the curtain at the end of act 1. Voltaire uses it to d'Argental to condemn Normandy's *parlement* that was criticising the king (D9119); to the author Palissot about a quarrel over a letter allegedly written by Diderot (D9058); to Élie de Beaumont about an eccentric legal decision concerning an inheritance (D16109); and he even uses this portmanteau phrase to Guy de Chabanon to describe the ructions unleashed by the publication of the atheist work *Système de la nature* (D16673). In this last case, the quotation seems to be in continuous prose in the letter, whereas in the previous three instances, it was set off as a line on its own, emphasising its status as a quotation.

This last example works because the line was well known and instantly recognised by Voltaire's correspondents. Sometimes, he announces his quotations: to Marie-Louise Denis (who has left him and whom he wants to feel sorry for him) he writes about his impending death (D14820):

---

[25] The original passage from Pascal: 'Et c'est pourquoi, toutes les fois qu'une proposition est inconcevable, il faut en suspendre le jugement et contraire; et si on le trouve manifestement faux, on peut hardiment affirmer la première, tout incompréhensible qu'elle est' (1992, p. 404).

Table 4.3 Seventeenth-century authors and their works quoted by
Voltaire in his letters

Racine (38 passages)
  Les Plaideurs (8)
  Phèdre (6)
  Andromaque (6)
  Bajazet (6)
  Mithridate (5)
  Britannicus (5)
  Bérénice (1)
  Athalie (1)
Boileau (36 passages)
  Art poétique (17)
  Epîtres (9)
  Satires (9)
  Le Lutrin (1)
Corneille (33 passages)
  La Mort de Pompée (6)
  Cinna (5)
  Pertharite (5)
  Héraclius (3)
  Othon (3)
  Polyeucte (3)
  Rodogune (2)
  Andromède (2)
  Le Cid (1)
  Don Sanche d'Aragon (1)
  Médée (1)
  Nicomède (1)
La Fontaine (27 passages)
  Fables (26)
  Le Songe de Vaux (1)
Molière (20 passages)
  Amphitryon (6)
  Le Misanthrope (4)
  Le Bourgeois gentilhomme (2)
  Le Tartuffe (2)
  Les Fourberies de Scapin (2)
  Monsieur de Pourceaugnac (1)
  L'Avare (1)
  Les Femmes savantes (1)
  Les Fâcheux (1)
Quinault (7 passages)
  Thésée (3)
  Atys (2)
  Proserpine (2)

> Vivez; je saurai bien mourir très
> honnêtement. Il y a plus de dix huit cent
> ans que Lucrèce a dit avant la Fontaine,
> Je voudrais qu'à cet âge
> On sortit de la vie ainsi que d'un banquet
> Remerciant son hôte et fesant son paquet.

> Live. I shall find a way to die well and honestly. It is over 1800
> years since Lucretius said, before La Fontaine, 'I would like at
> this age / to depart from life as from a banquet / thanking one's
> host and packing up one's bag.'

The quotation is from La Fontaine's *Fables* (8.1), 'La Mort et le mourant', and it recurs in letters to the marquise Du Deffand in 1769 (D15517) and to his great-nephew Dompierre d'Hornoy (D18806) – though in neither of these last two cases does Voltaire feel the need to name his source.

That Voltaire reuses quotations is not surprising. What does surprise is the number and variety of quotations that appear only once. From Molière's *Misanthrope* there are three different ones among the four that we identified (D1891, D4224, D6157, D12294). In the case of Corneille's Christian drama *Polyeucte*, we found three quoted passages, all different (D9492, D9959, D12302). Sometimes there are quotes, probably from memory, of texts familiar to the recipient of the letter (there is not much point in quoting something so obscure that it is not recognised). In writing to Jean Gabriel Le Bault, president of the Dijon *parlement* and, more importantly to Voltaire, supplier of fine burgundies, he begins by discussing a problem with one of the barrels supplied – the wine has turned bad – and then tactfully changes the subject to that of his woes concerning a legal battle with the president de Brosses over a small sum: 'Il n'a point voulu d'arbitres; et je commence à croire qu'il ne voudra point de juges, et qu'il abandonnera noblement cette importante affaire, où il s'agit du *foin que peut manger une poule en un jour*.' (He refused arbiters; and I am beginning to think that he will want no judges, and that he will nobly abandon this important business, which concerns *the straw that a chicken can eat in a day*) (D10193). The expression printed in italics makes clear that this is a quotation (underlined in the letter), but Besterman does not identify it, perhaps because it comes from the lesser-known comedy *Les Plaideurs* ('Du foin que peut manger une poule en un jour', 1.7). The power of the quotation is of course that it is an elegant put-down of the président de Brosses, and also that it comes from a comedy about the law, and he is writing to the senior magistrate in the Dijon *parlement*.

Often, Voltaire's verse quotations are set off in the text. In the case of this letter to d'Argental (D7014), the quotation 'Vous ne donnez qu'un jour, qu'une heure, qu'un moment' (you give but a day, but an hour, but a moment), from

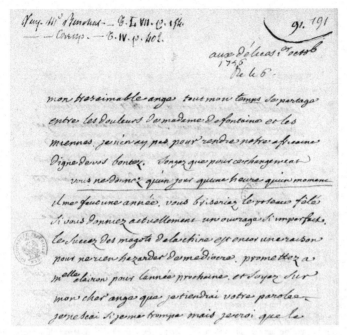

Figure 4.1 Manuscript letter D7014 (*quotation underlined*) https://gallica.bnf
.fr/ark:/12148/btv1b9064061w/f202.image

Racine's *Andromaque* (4.3) occurs on a separate line and its source is given by
Besterman. Figures 4.1, 4.2, and 4.3 show the gradual remediation of this letter
and its quotation from the original manuscript (Fig. 4.1), to Besterman's critical
edition (Fig. 4.2), and eventually online as part of *EE* (Fig. 4.3).[26]

In the case of a letter to the equally cultivated duc de Richelieu (D527), on the
other hand, a quotation from *Andromaque* (1.4) is run on in continuous prose,
with its twelve-syllable alexandrine rhythm the only clue that this is a quotation
(see Fig. 4.4): 'A de moindres faveurs des malheureux prétendent' (those out of
fortune seek lesser favours). Unsurprisingly, this embedded quotation is missed
by Besterman.

Likewise, a quotation from Racine's *Phèdre* (2.6), 'Dieux qui le connaissez, /
Est-ce donc la vertu que vous récompensez?' (Oh Gods who know him, is this
virtue that you reward?), occurs in a letter to the duc de Choiseul (D9147), and
again in the middle of a letter to D'Alembert (D14106, in which he is complain-
ing about the recognition given to Rousseau in England). In both cases, the two
lines are clearly a quotation and are set off in the text, though for reasons unclear
Besterman annotates the first example but not the second.

---

[26] On the remediation of new media objects, see Bolter & Grusin, 2000.

> *D7014. Voltaire to Charles Augustin Feriol,*
> *comte d'Argental*
>
> aux Délices 1er octob [1756]a
> Mon très aimable ange tout mon temps se partage entre les douleurs de
> madame de Fontaine et les miennes. Je n'en ay pas pour rendre notre afri-
> caine digne de vos bontez. Songez que pour ce changement
>
> *vous ne donne\[qu'un jour, qu'une heure, qu'un moment*1
>
> il me faut une année. Vous briseriez le roseau fêlé si vous donniez actuelle-
> ment un ouvrage si imparfait. Le succez des magots de la Chine est encor
> une raison pour ne rien hazarder de médiocre. Promettez à melle Clairon
> pour l'année prochaine, et soyez sûr mon cher ange que je tiendrai votre
> parole. Je ne sçai si je me trompe mais je croi que le vainqueur de Mahon
> gouvernera les comédiensb en 1757a. Alors vous aurez beau jeu. Attendez
> je vous en conjure ce temps favorable. J'espère que notre Zulime paraîtra
> alors avec *tous ses appas*a, et n'en parlera point. Il y a des choses essentielles à
> faire. C'est une maison dans la quelle il n'y a encor qu'un asséz bel apartement.
> J'avoue que madelle Clairon serait honnêtement logée, mais le reste serait au
> galetas. Laissez moy je vous en supplie travailler à rendre la maison supor-
> table. Je serai bientôt débarassé de cette histoire générale à la quelle je ne
> peux suffire. Un fardeau de plus me tuerait dans le triste état où je suis. Enfin
> je vous conjure par l'amitié que vous avez pour moy et qui fait la consolation
> de ma vie de ne rien précipiter. Je vous aurai autant d'obligation de cette
> précaution nécessaire, que je vous en ay de vos démarches auprès de mon
> héros.

Figure 4.2 Page image of letter D7014 from the Besterman critical edition

Sometimes Voltaire gives a nudge to his reader signalling a quotation, as when
he signs off a letter to Paul Moultou, 'La peste soit de l'orgueil et des orgueilleux,
comme La Flèche dit, la peste soit de l'avarice et des avaricieux!' (A plague on
pride and the proud, as La Flèche says, a plague on miserliness and misers!)
(D16069). The reference is to Molière's *L'Avare* (1.3), hinted at by his naming
La Flèche, the protagonist's servant. Similarly, he writes to the marquis de
Florian, 'mais il n'y a pas moyen d'envoyer après lui la justice en pleine mer,
comme dans les *Fourberies de Scapin*' (but there is no way of pursuing him with
justice on the high seas, as in the *Fourberies de Scapin*) (D20505) – a clear
reference to Molière's *Les Fourberies de Scapin* (2.7 and 3.3). Interestingly, he
alludes to the same passage in a letter to the baron de Grandcour, 'Je croi[s] qu'ils
seront un peu embarassés sur les côtés, et qu'ils auront de la peine à envoyer la
justice en pleine mer' (I think they will be somewhat embarrassed on the side, and
will struggle to pursue justice on the high seas) (D6717), but this time there is no
nudge to his reader (and Besterman does not annotate the reference).
Occasionally, Voltaire sets out to dazzle his reader with a quotation that he
knows to be unfamiliar, as when he opens a letter of 1752 to d'Argenson with a
long verse quotation, tentatively attributed (see Fig. 4.5).

aux Délices 1er octo^b[1756] ^{a}

Mon très aimable ange tout mon temps se partage entre les douleurs de madame de Fontaine et les miennes. Je n'en ay pas pour rendre notre africaine digne de vos bontez. Songez que pour ce changement

vous ne donnez qu'un jour, qu'une heure, qu'un moment[1]

il me faut une année. Vous briseriez le roseau fêlé si vous donniez actuellement un ouvrage si imparfait. Le succez des magots de la Chine est encor une raison pour ne rien hazarder de médiocre. Promettez à m^{elle} Clairon pour l'année prochaine, et soyez sûr mon cher ange que je tiendrai votre parole. Je ne sçai si je me trompe mais je croi que le vainqueur de Mahon gouvernera les comédiens^b en 1757[2]. Alors vous aurez beau jeu. Attendez je vous en conjure ce temps favorable. J'espère que notre Zulime paraîtra alors avec *tous ses appas*[3], et n'en parlera point. Il y a des choses essentielles à faire. C'est une maison dans la quelle il n'y a encor qu'un asséz bel apartement. J'avoue que mad^{elle} Clairon serait honnêtement logée, mais le reste serait au galetas. Laissez moy

Figure 4.3 Screenshot of letter D7014 (*EE*)

Even the highly cultured d'Argenson is unlikely to have known this passage, and the fact that Voltaire himself is mistaken in attributing the verses to Mellin de Saint-Gelais is proof of their obscurity – they are in fact by another bishop, the poet Jean Bertaut – but we know that Voltaire was especially drawn to these verses, as he recorded them in one of his notebooks (Voltaire, 1968–2021, vol. 81, p. 270–1, 274).

The two quotations of verse by Fontenelle are curious. To d'Argental, Voltaire writes (D20625):

> C'est une idée que je roule souvent dans ma tête, et qui me console.
> Et cette illusion pour quelque temps répare
> Le défaut des vrais biens que la nature avare
> N'a pas accordés aux humains.

> This is an idea I often turn over in my head and that consoles me / And for a time this illusion compensates / for the lack of true gifts that stingy nature / has denied human beings.

The verse is set off in the letter, but did Voltaire really expect his correspondent to identify this relatively obscure quotation from Fontenelle's *Poésies pastorales* (not identified by Besterman)? To Hennin, Voltaire sends a letter of

Partout où est la comédie, c'est là mon camp, et Zaire est mon général dont je suis volontiers les drapaux. Si vous pouviez me prêter une tente pour quelques jours dans votre maison sans que je vous incommodasse je vous serois très obligé. Je suis plus malade et plus chétif que jamais. Si j'allois vous trouver sur la Sambre en cet état, vous m'enverriez à l'hopital de l'armée. Je n'ay pas plus de santé qu'il m'en faut pour voir les grands yeux noirs de Zaïre, et je réserve pour elle le peu de vie que j'ay. La Sambre me tueroit, et la vue de Zaïre me ranime. M. Palu est je croi le maître de votre maison et soufrira bien que j'y aye un petit trou. Je me flatte, monseigneur, que votre santé est meilleur que jamais, que la fatigue qui me tueroit vous sied à merveille, que vous faites faire plus d'évolutions[1] que le chevalier Follard n'en a imaginées, et qu'avec tout cela vous serez charmé de revenir. Adieu, monseigneur, je suis le plus paresseux et le plus tendre de tous vos serviteurs. Je me flatte qu'un jour je passeray ma vie uniquement auprès de vous, et c'est une idée charmante pour moy. J'ay changé d'avis sur votre terre. A de moindres faveurs des malheureux prétendent. J'ay eu l'insigne folie de perdre près de douze mille francs chez la baronne et j'ay renoncé à être seigneur terrien. Aimez toujours votre adorateur.

V.

Figure 4.4 Screenshot of letter D527 (*EE, quotation highlighted*)

Electronic Enlightenment Scholarly Edition of Correspondence

Voltaire [François Marie Arouet] to Marc Pierre de Voyer de Paulmy, comte d'Argenson

Friday, 24 November 1752

DOCUMENT | ENCLOSURES | RELATED | VERSIONS | PARENT

A Postdam, 24 novembre 1752

Quand je revis ce que j'ai tant aimé,
Peu s'en fallut que mon feu rallumé
N'en fît le charme en mon âme renaître,
Et que mon cœur, autrefois son captif,
Ne ressemblât l'esclave fugitif,
A qui le sort fit rencontrer son maître.

C'est ce que disait, je crois, autrefois le saint évêque Saint Gelais[1], en rencontrant son ancienne maitresse; et j'en ai dit davantage en retrouvant vos anciennes bontés. Croyez, monseigneur, que vous n'êtes jamais sorti de mon cœur; mais je craignais que

Figure 4.5 Beginning of letter D5083 *(EE)*

extreme brevity: 'C'est aujourd'hui lundi que Monsieur Hennin doit avoir M. le Duc d'Aiguillon pour son ministre. Tout le reste est caché dans une nuit profonde' (It is today, Monday, that M. Hennin must have the Duc d'Aiguillon as his minister. All the rest is hidden in deepest night) (D17225).

Did Hennin even recognise that the second of the two sentences is spoken by an Oracle in *Thétis et Pélée* (3.8), an opera (*tragédie lyrique*) first performed in 1689, with a libretto by Fontenelle, and set to music by Pascal Collasse? It seems highly unlikely (and Besterman does not identify it as a quotation).

Voltaire is not simply an admirer of the French Classical age; he is widely acknowledged as its greatest historian, and in many letters he gives himself the role of literary critic and historian. He is militant, for example, in defending the cause of Philippe Quinault, best known as a librettist of operas, and now remembered for being singled out for criticism as a poet by Boileau. As a librettist, Quinault occupied a rather marginal position in the canon of seventeenth-century classicism, but Voltaire, who had no particular love of opera, had high regard for the quality of Quinault's verse and famously dissented from Boileau's condemnation of Quinault. The seven passages quoted in the letters testify to Voltaire's personal taste, as when he praises Quinault to D'Alembert, quoting from *Thésée* (3.7): 'Il est comme les diables dans Quinault: Goûtons l'unique bien des cœurs infortunés, / Ne soyons pas seuls misérables' (he is like the devils in Quinault: Let us enjoy the only benefit of unhappy hearts, Let us not be unhappy alone) (D12296). To d'Olivet (D13807) and La Harpe (D17702) he likewise praises Quinault, always using quotations to support his argument. There are many such letters in which Voltaire discusses books and plays, in which the quotations form the subject matter: the many letters to d'Argental in which he discusses his own plays, or a 1761 letter to Duclos, connected with his publication of the *Commentaires sur Corneille* (D10229), or again when he writes to Cideville in 1761, pointing out, with supporting quotations, his discovery that Racine's *Andromaque* is partially indebted to Corneille's *Pertharite* (D10037). The literary historian in Voltaire is shaped by his being a purveyor of quotations.

4.5 Quoting His Contemporaries

There are fewer instances in which Voltaire quotes contemporary authors, in part for the obvious reason that his contemporaries had not yet acquired 'classic' status (leaving aside the case of Voltaire himself). The one exception is Jean-Baptiste Rousseau, whose *Odes* Voltaire quotes on three occasions, in letters to Cideville (D593), Charles Bordes (D13699), and Frederick II (D18768).

Sometimes Voltaire quotes the writing of his correspondent as a way of showing his appreciation. When the dramatist La Noue sends his play *Mahomet second* to Voltaire for comment, it is not surprising that Voltaire's letter in reply includes verses from the play (D1966). He similarly quotes Duclos's *Histoire de Louis IX* in a letter to the author in 1745 (D3102). When

Voltaire writes to Nivelle de La Chaussée, he flatters the poet by quoting his *Épître de Clio* back to him (D1070). In this way, Voltaire can use the correspondence as a means of conducting literary criticism.

On the occasion of the posthumous publication of Helvétius' *De l'Homme* in 1772, Voltaire writes first to D'Alembert in July 1773 (D18450), including several citations from the work, and then, in November 1773 to the marquise Du Deffand (D18607) on the same subject, quoting several passages for her appreciation. His remarks following these citations give us an interesting insight into one use of selected quotation; Voltaire in effect provides his friends with a 'reader's digest' of a recent publication (relieving them of the need to read the book for themselves):

> Je prends ces petits diamants au hasard, Madame. Il y en a mille dans ce goût dont l'éclat m'a frappé. Cela n'empêche pas que le livre ne soit très mauvais. Je passe ma vie à chercher des pierres précieuses dans du fumier, et quand j'en rencontre je les mets à part et j'en fais mon profit. C'est par là que les mauvais livres sont quelquefois très utiles.

> I pick these small gems at random, Madame. There are a thousand like this whose sparkle struck me. That does not alter the fact that the book is very bad. I spend my life searching in manure for precious stones, and when I find them, I set them to one side and make use of them. In this way bad books are sometimes very useful.

When Saint-Lambert publishes his poetic masterpiece *Les Saisons* in 1769, he sends an advance copy to Voltaire, who mentions and cites the work in his reply (D15504). Voltaire then cites the poem with great enthusiasm in a remarkable letter to Du Pont de Nemours that combines citations of both Saint-Lambert and Boileau (D15679). When Saint-Lambert sends a new edition of the poem in 1774, Voltaire responds again using quotations (D18534), as ever in praise.

On other occasions, Voltaire quotes to criticise: his enmity for fellow tragedian Crébillon père is well known, and he quotes him on two occasions, not flatteringly (D9959, D19016). He is never kind about Jean-Jacques Rousseau, and he quotes him in four letters, commenting on *La Nouvelle Héloïse* to d'Olivet (D9566), on the *Lettres écrites de la montagne* in a letter to Tronchin (D12262), on the *Contrat social* to Pierre de Taulès (D13657), and finally, on the *Lettre à Beaumont* in a letter to David Hume (D13623).

In promoting the work and the cause of his fellow *philosophes*, quotation can be useful. When Voltaire hears from D'Alembert that Marmontel's *Bélisaire* had been condemned by the Sorbonne in 1767, he writes to the author in May of that year (D14184) using the quotation given to him by D'Alembert: 'La vérité brille de sa propre lumière, et l'on n'éclaire pas les esprits avec la flamme des bûchers' (Truth shines with its own light, and you cannot illuminate minds with the burning stake) (D14161). Voltaire reuses this same quotation the same day in a letter to Paul Rabaut (D14185), and again two days later to Mme Du Deffand (D14187). Besterman leaves these last two instances of quotation unattributed. In a 1751 letter to Hénault, Voltaire refers to D'Alembert's preface to the *Encyclopédie*, quoting what he calls 'these remarkable words': 'On nuit plus au progrès de l'esprit en plaçant mal les récompenses qu'en les supprimant' (We do more harm to the progress of the human mind in rewarding wrongly than in suppressing rewards) (D4618). In a letter to Maupeou in November 1772, when the minister was actively engaged in his reform programme, Voltaire quotes d'Argenson's *Considérations sur le gouvernement ancien et présent de la France* (D18033). Quotation in Voltaire's hands can be a useful political weapon.

4.6 Final Thoughts

Our digital reading of Voltaire's quotations has clearly led us to new insights, but there are also limits to the methodology. We have confined ourselves to instances where a tangible quotation of another work is found in the correspondence; as we said at the outset, Voltaire often mentions works simply by the name of their title or author, but this would require another sort of reading technique. In some cases, Besterman's own index of sources identifies quotations that sequence alignment missed, for example a paraphrase of Racine's *Andromaque* (1.2) in D18156 – this is because the passage is short, and in Besterman's words, 'adapted', from the original, thus causing it to fall outside our matching parameters.

Furthermore, there are certainly sources that we missed based on the scope and nature of the ARTFL-Frantext database: for example, it does not include La Fontaine's verse tales, the *Contes et nouvelles en vers*, a favourite work of Voltaire's and a particular influence on his own verse *contes*. The results are also inconsistent, and potentially misleading if one does not sometimes check them with other resources. For instance, in the long letter from Voltaire to the abbé d'Olivet, already mentioned (D9959), Voltaire cites two passages from Crébillon *père*, a contemporary tragedian and famous rival:

> [...] J'ai dit et j'ai dû dire combien sont horribles à la fois et ridicules ces
>   autres vers que nous avons entendu réciter au théâtre:
> Chacun a ses vertus, ainsi qu'il a ses dieux.
> Le sceptre absout toujours la main la plus coupable.
> Le crime n'est forfait que pour les malheureux.
> Oui, lorsque de nos soins la justice est l'objet,
> Elle y doit emprunter le secours du forfait, etc. ...
> On ne peut dire plus mal des choses plus infâmes et plus sottes [...].

[…] I have said and I must have said how horrible and ridiculous are those other lines that we have heard recited on stage:

Each has his virtues, as he has his gods / the sceptre always absolves the guiltiest hand. / Crime is an infraction only for the unfortunate. Yes, when justice is the object of our cares / it must borrow help from crime, etc. … More despicable and silly things could not be expressed more badly […].

The second quotation ('Oui … '), taken from *Sémiramis*, is identified by our algorithm. The former, however, was missed, because it comes from Crébillon's play *Xerxès*, which – for unknown reasons – is not part of the Frantext database. These sorts of lacunae are to be expected, given the overly canonical nature of the Frantext corpus. This is also more than likely the reason for which we found so many more Latin quotations than French: Voltaire was not necessarily quoting Latin texts with more frequency, but the French texts that he did refer to again and again – beyond the Classical repertoire that he knew by heart and that forms our modern canon – might well come from 'lesser' works that have not yet been included in the Frantext corpus. There is an obvious danger of concluding that Voltaire has overly canonical tastes, when in fact we may be missing some of his more recondite, and therefore more interesting, references precisely because our database is too canonical.

There is a further problem that has to do with how we pre-process texts; for large-scale text comparisons, we remove 'stopwords' (overly common and function words) before generating n-grams – those sequences of n words that co-occur – which reduces the dimensionality of the comparison algorithm and saves time computationally (Olsen et al., 2011). However, if Voltaire is citing (as he often does) shorter verses with a high number of 'stopwords', the algorithm will fail to find a match. For example, in a letter to Pierre de Belloy in 1765 (D12512), Voltaire cites two lines from Belloy's *Siège de Calais*. In the first line, there are only two substantive words left to form an n-gram, 'forcez' and 'seigneur', which means that our pre-defined three–n-gram threshold is not met (see note 24 above); this is also the case with the second line, where only 'étranger' and 'patrie' are retained (Voltaire's quotations are italicised):

Vous me forcez? Seigneur, d'être plus grand que vous
Vous me forcez, seigneur, d'etre plus grand que vous

You force me, my lord, to be greater than you

Plus je vis d'étrangers, plus j'aimai ma patrie
Plus je vis l'étranger, plus j'aimai ma patrie

The more strangers I met, the more I loved my native land
The more I saw the stranger […]

This is a function of the 'noise reduction' needed for the algorithm to work at scale, meaning we could ask for more finer-grained matches but would get much more noise than signal and likely explode the time needed to generate matches.

Notwithstanding these inevitable limitations, this experiment has advanced our understanding in a number of ways. The Besterman edition fails to annotate a surprisingly large number of the passages discussed here; in some cases this is understandable given the relative obscurity of the quotation, such as the two passages from Fontenelle's verse (D17225, D20625). But he also misses better-known authors, such as the quotation from Racine's *Les Plaideurs* (D10193) and the one from Racine's *Andromaque* (D527, in this last case, perhaps because it runs on in the prose of the letter and is not set off). The work carried out here will enable us in due course to revise the digital edition of the correspondence and to augment its annotation, making it fuller and more consistent: at the moment, the same quote from Racine's *Phèdre* is annotated in D9147 but not in D14106.

The quotations examined in this section have intrinsic interest for what they tell us about Voltaire but also when studied as a structured whole. In enhancing the digital edition and in making it possible for these references to be linked to each other, we shall be able to interrogate the database in a wholly new manner. We have seen how one quotation, 'Ma foi, juge et plaideurs, il faudroit tout lier', from *Les Plaideurs*, is found four times in the correspondence. By linking these quotations together, we create another way of thinking about this edifice: a digital edition could effect these links and open up other ways of reading the letters which would follow the trails laid by Voltaire's literary allusiveness. A more expansive database project, *Digital Voltaire*, incorporating all the works in addition to the letters, is currently under construction, and this will make it possible further to link these quotations to Voltaire's notebooks, the titles of the books in his library, the extensive marginalia contained in many of those books, and so forth.

Even the present findings give us new insights into how Voltaire thinks and writes. Many of the quotations are slightly inaccurate, which is only to be expected since in most cases he is presumably quoting from memory. When he writes to d'Argenson with a long quotation that he (wrongly) attributes to Mellin de Saint-Gelais (D5083), we may posit that he has taken the trouble to copy out the quotation – especially as the extract is copied in one of his notebooks; but in most cases, when a line from *Andromaque* finds itself woven into the prose of a letter (D527), Voltaire is clearly drawing on the vast stock of quotations in his personal memory bank. This experiment has increased our knowledge about the number of authors and works that Voltaire knows well enough to quote – and apparently often knows well enough to quote by heart.

In the classical tradition, Voltaire has read and absorbed the canonical works to the point where he quotes even perhaps without fully realising it. In his critical edition of Voltaire's epic poem *La Henriade* (Voltaire, 1968–2021, vol. 2), Owen Taylor gives in his footnotes lines of Racine and Corneille that seem to underlie 'original' verses of the poem – a good instance of Voltaire's memory bank in action. In a letter of 1738, Voltaire advises Helvétius about the difficulties of writing good verse: 'Je vous donne un bon conseil après vous avoir donné de bien mauvais exemples' (I am giving you some good advice after having given you some really bad examples) (D1673). It is impossible here not to recall a maxim of the seventeenth-century aphorist La Rochefoucauld, 'Les vieillards aiment à donner de bons préceptes, pour se consoler de n'être plus en état de donner de mauvais exemples' (Old men like to offer wise guidance, as consolation for no longer being able to give bad examples) – though whether this is a conscious or an unconscious echo on the part of Voltaire would be hard to say with certainty. His store of memorised quotations is a fundamental part of his literary culture that colours his writing and shapes his judgement as a literary critic. Writing to Condorcet in 1776, he discusses the writings of La Harpe and Desfontaines, talks of Chamfort, praises Racine for the harmony of his verse, then, quoting a line of Tibullus in Latin, he poses his correspondent a direct question:

> A propos, il faut que vous jugiez entre le duc de La Rochefoucauld et Confucius, qui des deux a le mieux défini la gravité. Le seigneur français a dit, la gravité est un mystère de corps inventé pour cacher les défauts de l'esprit. Le seigneur chinois a dit, la gravité n'est que l'écorce de la sagesse, mais elle la conserve.

> By the way, you must judge between La Rochefoucault and Confucius, as to which of the two best defined seriousness. The French lord said that serious-ness is a mystery of the body invented to hide the shortcomings of the spirit. The Chinese lord said that seriousness is only the shell of wisdom, but it conserves it. (D20453)

This letter is a literary tour de force, and its 82-year-old author seems to have absolute recall of the authors he has read and often memorised. In the end, the digital readings in this section help us to explore further the riches of Voltaire's memory bank.

5 Quotations | Latin

5.1 Introduction

As we have just seen, Voltaire likes quoting literary texts in his letters; French classics are present in abundance, but also a fair number of Latin texts and authors. Reading through the correspondence, one gets the strong sense that

Voltaire is often quoting these authors from memory, the mark of his Jesuit teachers no doubt, who put Latin at the centre of their pedagogy. Latin texts, and in particular Latin poetry, formed the cornerstone of the curriculum for the Jesuit colleges in the seventeenth and eighteenth centuries in France (Dainville, 1978; Fumaroli, 2003). At the Louis-le-Grand college, Voltaire benefited from the teaching of some of the most renowned Jesuit college, in particular, Fr Porée, who famously taught a 'Senecan' (i.e. tight and concise) prose style, and Fr Thoulier (later the abbé d'Olivet), a noted Cicero scholar, who would become a lifelong friend to Voltaire and one of his key literary correspondents.

Latin verse played a preponderant role in the Jesuit curriculum. As such, the major Latin poets were at the heart of teaching and learning: Virgil, Ovid, and Horace were the big three, of course, a well-established pedagogical canon that went back to the sixteenth century at least (Dainville, 1978, p. 171). In practical terms, the Jesuits taught by way of daily recitals (*recitatio*) of memorised verse by all students: 'On attachait à la *recitatio* une importance dont nous n'avons pas idée aujourd'hui' (The *recitatio* was accorded an importance that is hard for us to fathom today) (Dainville, 1978, p. 175). Students were thus required to commit large chunks of Latin verse to memory as a regular practice. Furthermore, the Jesuits firmly believed that these acts of memorisation served as the most efficient means of retaining and recalling information. Voltaire himself comments on this practice when describing the Jesuit Claude Buffier, author of a book entitled *Mémoire artificielle* (Artificial memory), in his 'catalogue' of seventeenth-century writers: 'Il a fait servir les vers (je ne dis pas la poésie) à leur premier usage, qui était d'imprimer dans la mémoire des hommes les événements dont on voulait garder le souvenir' (He made verse (which is not to say poetry) serve its primary purpose, which was to imprint in men's memory the events that one wanted to remember) (Voltaire, 1968–2021, vol. 12, p. 72). This Jesuit pedagogy no doubt left its mark on the young Arouet and reappears time and again throughout his life's work. This section aims to uncover and explore these traces and the social manner in which Voltaire deploys Latin quotations over the entirety of his correspondence.

Our recourse to digital tools and resources to examine Voltaire's use of Latin is perhaps best demonstrated by an anecdote. When preparing a paperback anthology of Voltaire's letters (Voltaire, 2017), we were faced with a letter with a Latin quotation that required a note: 'Ornari res ipsa negat, contenta doceri' (the subject requires no ornament, it suffices that it is taught) (D1666). The Besterman edition gives no reference for this quotation, merely a misleading attribution to a seventeenth-century treatise on painting by Dufresnoy, which the editor openly cribs from the 1832 Beuchot edition: 'Beuchot [...] ingeniously quotes "Ornari præcepta negant" from Charles Alphonse Dufresnoy,

De arte graphica.' And yet now, with a simple Internet search, it is an easy matter to identify the passage in a matter of seconds – the quotation is from Manilius' *Astronomica* no less. How many other such passages were lurking in the correspondence, we wondered? And what might they tell us about Voltaire's formidable Latin culture?

5.2 The Experiment

On the whole, Besterman manages to identify passages when they are from the major Latin writers (Horace, Virgil, Ovid, Lucretius, etc.) – that is, the authors for whom there were concordances easily available in the 1950s and 1960s. In the case of lesser poets like Manilius, however, where no concordance was available, Besterman was obliged to leave the passages unannotated. These quotations can now be easily identified thanks to the availability of comprehensive collections of Latin literature and new digital methods for identifying similar passages across datasets. More generally, identifying Voltaire's use and reuse of classical authors enlarges the list of writers one traditionally assumes Voltaire had at his fingertips, and changes, perhaps radically, our sense of the breadth and depth of his Latin and humanist culture. Truly to understand his practice as a writer, we needed a way of dealing with what amounts to his own equivalent of big data.

Using the TextPAIR sequence alignment algorithm described in Section 4.2 (Olsen et al., 2011; Roe, 2012), here we describe a similar attempt to study, through the use of quotations, the dynamic presence of the Latin literary tradition in Voltaire's letters. To begin, we identified some 854 Latin quotations in Voltaire's correspondence by comparing his letters to the Packard Humanities Institute's Classical Latin Texts (PHI) digital corpus.[27] The PHI contains essentially all Latin literary texts written before AD 200, as well as some texts selected from later antiquity. The resulting alignments allowed us to move beyond Besterman's ad hoc manner of identifying quotations and towards a more systematic understanding of Voltaire's use (and reuse) of Latin authors.

First, however, we needed to winnow down the number of initial matches: of the more than 800 quotations identified, many are repeated via multiple authors, thus skewing our results upwards. This speaks to the culture of quotation and reuse that permeated the ancients, and that was subsequently passed down through the Renaissance humanist tradition and then, finally, on to Voltaire (Goyet, 1996). This is especially true of the several commentators from Late Antiquity included in the PHI corpus, most notably the grammarians Servius, Porphyrio, Aulus Gellius, Terentianus, and Aemilius Asper, all of whom cited

---

[27] https://latin.packhum.org/.

Table 5.1 342 individual Latin passages found in letters by Voltaire

Author	Number of quotations
Horace	175
Virgil	92
Ovid	39
Lucretius	12
Terence	6
Cicero	4
Juvenal	3
Petronius	2
Phaedrus	2
Lucan	2
Persius	2
Manilius	1
Statius	1
Cato the Elder	1

earlier Latin poets in their works. By eliminating these false positive matches, we moved from 854 total citations (Voltaire and his correspondents included) to a more manageable 342 individual Latin quotations used in letters written by Voltaire himself (see Table 5.1).

The quoted authors are overwhelmingly poets, and the fact that Horace, Virgil, and Ovid form the top three is not at all surprising, though the presence of Horace is unquestionably dominant. The list, however, goes beyond the usual suspects: Manilius, Statius, and Cato the Elder are hardly canonical authors, and their presence is interesting, especially if Voltaire is quoting them from memory. In all, there is breadth as well as depth in this list of authors, attesting to Voltaire's deep investment in perpetuating and revivifying the Latin literary tradition.

5.3 The Latin Network

The next important question we confronted had less to do with *who* Voltaire was quoting and rather more to do with *to whom* these quotations were addressed. To put it another way: who, exactly, were the recipients of letters containing Latin quotations, and what, if anything, can we make of them as a 'group' or subset of Voltaire's correspondents? In all we found 101 different recipients of at least some Latin, out of a total 1,465 recipients in Voltaire's correspondence (or roughly 6.8 per cent). This is quite small as a proportion of addressees overall.

Table 5.2 'Procope' intellectual and social network categories

Knowledge Networks	
Letters_Literary	[the broadest category of writers, poets, playwrights, grammarians, critics, authors, etc., who may write on history, theatre, travel, music, art …]
Letters_Philosophical	[specifically for interest in philosophy]
Letters_Religious	[all writers on religious matters]
Political Economy	[economist, political theorist, sociologist, political reformer]
Sciences	[the broadest category, for unspecified interests]
Sciences_Natural	[biological, natural history, zoology, botany, chemistry, agriculture, mineralogy, entomology, ornithology, etc.; includes alchemy]
Sciences_Mathematical	[physics, astronomy, calculus, geometry, mathematics, etc.]
Sciences_Medicine	[physiology, anatomy, etc.]
Social Networks	
Elite	[anyone whose function (e.g., minister, chancellor) or elevated social status (i.e., aristocracy, great wealth) places them in the elite segment of society; what in eighteenth-century France was known as *le monde*]
Aristocracy	[anyone who is part of the nobility or gentry]
Court	[individuals who live in and through a court]
Government	[anyone who works directly for the state, including judges, diplomats, and all other officials; with the exception of military]
Military	[officers, soldiers, navy]

So how can we gloss these names as members of a group, or network, of readers of Latin quotations? In order to address this question somewhat sociologically, we cross-referenced our results with the 'Procope' prosopographical ontology and dataset of 'French correspondents of major Enlightenment figures' developed at Stanford (Cosma et al., 2016; see Table 5.2).[28]

---

[28] The dataset merges metadata from *Electronic Enlightenment* for the French correspondents of important Enlightenment figures (including Voltaire, Rousseau, Hume, and Smith) with metadata from the Groupe d'Alembert concerning D'Alembert's French correspondents. These data were subsequently enriched by a group of researchers at (or formerly at) Stanford: Maria Comsa,

Using these two sets of metadata (e.g., the names of those who received Latin passages from Voltaire and their subsequent place in the Procope ontology), we were able to automatically assign social network categories to the majority of recipients on our list, with those few non-French addressees like Frederick II being assigned to categories manually. While the dataset admittedly has its limitations, including an overlapping hierarchy that somewhat muddles quantitative analysis, its availability as an open data project is to be lauded and allowed us a means of quickly evaluating our results, revealing the fundamentally 'elite' status of this subset of Voltaire's correspondents (see Table 5.3).

Table 5.3 Top twenty recipients of Latin quotations from Voltaire

Letter recipient	Number of quotations	'Procope' networks
Frederick II	41	Aristocracy, Elite, Government
Thiriot	38	Letters_Literary
Cideville	29	Elite, Government
Francesco Algarotti	18	Aristocracy, Letters
D'Alembert	15	Letters_Philosophical, Sciences
D'Argental	14	Aristocracy, Elite, Government
Jean-Baptiste-Nicolas Formont	14	Government, Letters_Literary
François Joachim, cardinal de Bernis	12	Aristocracy, Elite, Government
D'Olivet	11	Letters_Literary
René Louis de Voyer de Paulmy	10	Aristocracy, Elite, Government
Helvétius	9	Court, Sciences_Medicine
Élie Bertrand	8	Clergy, Letters, Sciences_Natural
Turgot	7	Aristocracy, Elite, Government
Francesco Albergati Capacelli	7	Aristocracy, Letters_Literary
Jean-Jacques Le Franc de Pompignan	7	Aristocracy, Elite, Government

Melanie Conroy, Dan Edelstein, Chloe Edmondson, and Claude Willan. See https://exhibits.stanford.edu/data/catalog/bc436tm1194.

Table 5.3 (cont.)

Letter recipient	Number of quotations	'Procope' networks
Claude Etienne Darget	7	Government
Claude Philippe Fyot de La Marche	7	Aristocracy, Elite, Government
Charles Palissot de Montenoy	7	Letters_Literary
Cosimo Alessandro Collini	6	Aristocracy, Letters_Literary
Dompierre d'Hornoy	5	Aristocracy, Government

As Table 5.3 indicates, the overwhelming majority of recipients of Latin quotations from Voltaire come either directly from the high aristocracy, government, or military, or are men of letters or philosophers tied in some way to these same social networks. A small subgroup of those in the liberal and medical professions, as well as high and low clergy, round out this list of recipients of Latin quotations (see Table 5.4).

Gender is an obvious factor: all addressees are male apart from one. Given that men generally learned Latin and women did not, the reason for the gendered use of Latin quotations is self-evident. This is further reinforced by the manner in which Voltaire uses two verses from Virgil with the duchesse de Choiseul, his single female addressee, in a letter from 1771:

> Pour moi, Madame, qui les aime passionément je vous dirai
> Ante leves ergo pascentur in æthere cervi
> Quam nostro illius labatur pectore vultus.
> Vous entendez le latin, Madame, vous savez ce que celà veut dire:
> Les cerfs iront paître dans l'air avant que j'oublie son visage.

> For me, Madame, who loves them [Theocritus and Virgil] passionately, I shall say […]. You understand Latin, Madame, and you know what this means: The deer will be grazing in the heavens before I forget his face. (D17251)

After quoting the two lines from the *Bucolics*, Voltaire goes on to translate them immediately for Madame de Choiseul, even though she can perhaps understand the Latin – a flagrant case of early-modern mansplaining.

Elsewhere among the 101 addressees, there is a clearly defined social group of old, close friends from Voltaire's time at school, namely those with whom he had learned Latin, including the marquis d'Argenson (later foreign minister), the comte d'Argenson (later war minister), the duc de Richelieu (soldier and

Table 5.4 'Procope' social and intellectual networks of recipients of Latin quotations[29]

'Procope' network	Number of recipients
Letters_Literary	40
Government	39
Aristocracy	31
Elite	27
Court	8
Letters_Philosophical	6
Clergy	6
Sciences_Mathematical	5
Military	5
Lawyer	4
Sciences_Medicine	3
Letters	3
Sciences_Natural	2
Letters_Religious	2
Sciences	1

leading courtier), d'Argental (lawyer in the Paris *parlement*), and Pierre-Robert Le Cornier de Cideville (lawyer in the Rouen *parlement*). There is also as an overlapping subgroup in Normandy, which includes connections from Voltaire's early legal career, including Jean-Baptiste de Formont, a wealthy, talented light poet who was also friends with Cideville, and Thiriot, an early friend of Voltaire's from when they were both young apprentice lawyers, who was also friends with Formont and Cideville.

Otherwise, we find many cultivated acquaintances in this group who are themselves authors: Frederick II, Algarotti, D'Alembert, and others; along with the abbé d'Olivet, who, in addition to having been Voltaire's teacher, was translator of Cicero and Demosthenes into French and elected to a seat at the Académie française in 1723. Clearly, Voltaire's use of Latin was determined by his readership. But also, by constructing an epistolary community with selected groups of correspondents, Voltaire underscored their shared experiences and humanist culture.

5.4 Latin as Exchange Currency

To what extent was this sort of cultural exchange reciprocal? In other words, if Voltaire writes to you quoting Latin poets, do you feel obliged to respond in

---

[29] Obviously, there are more than 101 labels attributed here, which is explained by the fact that addressees can belong to more than one category.

kind? What does it mean, for instance, that Voltaire uses Latin in so many letters to Frederick, yet the king rarely uses Latin in return? And what about people like François-Louis Allamand, Jean-Gabriel de La Touche, and Marmontel, who use a fair amount of Latin in their letters but receive none in return from Voltaire? To respond to these queries, we identified the forty-one correspondents who sent at least one Latin quotation to Voltaire (either reciprocated or not), a list (see Table 5.5) that is surprisingly distinct from the recipients.

Socially, the forty-one respondents identified belong, by and large, to the same 'elite' categories of government or aristocracy, although there is a markedly greater presence of *hommes de lettres* (literary figures; a 'knowledge network' that overlaps with the 'social networks' drawn from 'Procope') in this second list (see Table 5.6).

Jean-Jacques Rousseau, for instance, never on the friendliest terms with Voltaire, includes two separate quotations from Cicero – an author whom Voltaire quotes surprisingly little – in his long response to Voltaire's poem on the Lisbon earthquake (D6973). These quotations, both drawn from the *De Senectute*, represent the only Latin passages in Rousseau's more than 6,000-word letter and serve to support the Genevan's defence of providentialism. This manner of using the ancients to advance modern philosophical arguments is well documented in the eighteenth century (see Edelstein, 2008; Norman, 2011), and Rousseau is clearly trading on established practices in his attempt to shift Voltaire's attitude towards Optimism. Unfortunately, aside from a brief letter of reply from Voltaire in September 1756 (D6993), the epistolary exchange between the two *philosophes* comes to a halt, and we are left to wonder if Voltaire might otherwise have marshalled his own set of Latin quotations as a retort.

Latin quotes thus become a sort of common cultural currency on which Voltaire, and those in his correspondence network, trade. The best quotes have a long shelf life and can occur at almost any period, from Voltaire's early days as a lawyer to his final months in Paris. Take the famous line from Virgil's *Aeneid*, 'macte nova virtute, puer, sic itur ad astra' (congratulations, boy, on your new-found manly courage; this is the way to the stars) (9.641). In a 1732 letter to Cideville (D503), Voltaire 'adapts' (to use Besterman's term) the line to read 'Macte animo, generose puer, sic itur ad astra' (Congratulations, noble boy, this is the way to the stars). Far from a simple adaptation, however, Voltaire's line is actually a mash-up of two separate quotations: 'Macte animo iuvenis!' (Bless your mind, noble boy) from Statius' *Thebaid* (7.280) and the second part of Virgil's original verse (all the more complicated, because 'macte' has more than one meaning in Latin). Voltaire reuses his hybrid quotation in 1736 with the marquis d'Argens (D1228) and then the truncated 'macte animo'

Table 5.5 Correspondents who send more than one Latin quotation to Voltaire

Respondent	Passages	Reciprocated	'Procope' network
D'Alembert	20	Yes	Letters_Philosophical, Mathematical
Paul Desforges-Maillard	13	Yes	Government, Letters_Literary
François Louis Allamand	10	No	Clergy, Letters_Literary, Philosophical
Charles de Brosses	9	Yes	Aristocracy, Government
La Touche	9	No	Elite, Commerce
Thiriot	7	Yes	Letters_Literary
Francesco Algarotti	6	Yes	Aristocracy, Letters
Marmontel	5	No	Government, Letters_Literary
Louis-René de La Chalotais	5	Yes	Elite, Government, Letters_Religious
Turgot	5	Yes	Aristocracy, Elite, Government
d'Olivet	5	Yes	Letters_Literary
Dupont	4	Yes	Letters_Literary
François-Augustin de Barneville	3	No	Military
Cideville	3	Yes	Elite, Government
Adrien Blin de Sainmore	3	No	Letters_Literary
Samuel Pechell	3	No	Lawyer
César de Missy	2	No	Letters_Literary
Johann Rudolf Sinner	2	No	Letters_Literary
Gregorio Mayáns y Siscar	2	No	Letters_Literary
Gabriel-Henri Gaillard	2	No	Letters_Literary
Jean-Jacques Rousseau	2	No	Letters_Literary, Letters_Philosophical
Francesco Albergati Capacelli	2	Yes	Aristocracy, Letters_Literary
Frederick II	2	Yes	Aristocracy, Elite, Government

Table 5.6 'Procope' social and intellectual networks of correspondents who send Latin to Voltaire

'Procope' network	Number of senders
Letters_Literary	22
Government	14
Aristocracy	9
Elite	8
Letters_Philosophical	3
Lawyer	2
Commerce	2
Clergy	2
Sciences_Mathematical	1
Military	1
Letters_Religious	1
Letters_Antiquarian	1
Letters	1
Court	1

by itself to Helvétius in 1738 (D1521), which Besterman annotates as 'an echo of Virgil', but that in reality comes from Statius. Voltaire goes on to use the quotation (sometimes truncated, but mostly in full) eleven more times from 1738 to 1775, which makes its way from Helvétius, to Frederick II, D'Alembert, and La Harpe, among others. The currency of the quotation even goes on to outlive its maker: Chateaubriand quotes this 'altered passage' of Virgil twice in his *Mémoires d'outre-tombe*, and Dumas père does likewise in his *Ange Pitou* (1851). And today, Voltaire's 'macte animo! Generose puer sic itur ad astra' lives on as the (rather macho) motto of the Brazilian Air Force Academy (see Fig. 5.1). Voltaire's global reach as a writer never ceases to surprise.

Other, better-known quotations, such as Terence's 'homo sum, humani nil a me alienum puto' (*Heauton Timorumenos*, 1, 1.77), circulated widely during the Enlightenment (Delon, 1984), and Voltaire's role is more as disseminator than originator. Some quotations, while repeated, have a more intimate connotation and are limited to certain correspondents. Another line from the *Aeneid* (I.630), for example, 'non ignara mali miseris succurrere disco' (no stranger to misfortune myself, I have learned to relieve the sufferings of others) – which coincidentally plays an important role in Rousseau's *Emile* – is used by Voltaire to express empathy regarding an undisclosed illness to Joseph de Menoux in 1754 (D5749), before being reused in his first letter to a young admirer, Charles Palissot (D6608, 1755), in much the same manner. Twenty-three years later,

Figure 5.1 Logo of the Brazilian Air Force Academy

upon his arrival in Paris, on what will be his final visit, Voltaire uses the quotation again to Palissot (D21059) and commits to reread the latter's works for consolation on what will soon be his deathbed. Here, over the course of two decades and not a few controversies surrounding Palissot and the *philosophes*, Voltaire's recourse to Virgil effectively bookends a more than forty-letter correspondence as a way of affirming their friendship and shared culture, and in the meantime bridging their philosophical differences.

5.5 Final Thoughts

These are just some of the preliminary results that we have begun to process in the context of a larger project on Voltaire's culture of text reuse (including his penchant for 'self-plagiarism' – see Cronk, 2007). As with most digital humanities projects, initial computational analyses do not always produce 'clean' results or cut-and-dried interpretations: some of the results have to be examined carefully, and some – as was the case for the grammarians and commentators mentioned above – will prove spurious or misleading. One begins by asking one set of questions – can we identify Voltaire's use of Latin and verify Besterman's attributions? – and end up with new ones (e.g., with whom did Voltaire use Latin, and how?). Equally, we could extend these questions by examining other literary quotations (e.g., from French or Italian authors) and by including other correspondence collections, comparing Diderot's or Rousseau's use of Latin, for instance, to that of Voltaire.

Ideally, this sort of experimental research approach also generates *new* research questions, ones that would have been difficult to frame outside of the digital environment. In this case, we were quickly confronted with the notion of what constitutes an instance of 'reuse' as opposed to an allusion or a more oblique cultural reference. For example, our algorithm identified this passage from Cicero's epistles (underlining added):

> Vale. CICERO BASILO S. Tibi gratulor, mihi gaudeo. te amo, tua tueor. a te amari et quid agas quidque agatur certior fieri volo.

> I congratulate you, I rejoice for myself. I love you, I look out for your interests. I want to be loved by you and I want to be informed as to what you are doing and what is being done.

as a potential reuse by Voltaire in a letter to Marmontel from 1749:

> Si vous recevez ma lettre ce soir, vous pourrez m'envoyer votre poulet pour M. de Richelieu, que je ferai partir sur le champ. Te amo, tua tueor, te diligo, te plurimum, &c.

> If you receive my letter this evening, you can send me your chicken for M. de Richelieu, which I shall dispatch immediately. [in Latin:] I love you, I look out for your interests, I love you very much, etc. (D3918)

Is this reuse or not? Besterman makes no mention of Cicero in his annotation but rather places this passage into a more generic class of 'Roman epistolary formulas'. But perhaps there is more going on here; perhaps the model of Cicero's epistles – central to the Jesuit syllabus – remains at the forefront of Voltaire's mind when he himself is writing letters. With the sorts of addressees to whom he uses Latin quotations, he may likewise use a Ciceronian subscription. It seems clear that in a case such as this, the Ciceronian model shapes Voltaire's epistolary rhetoric.

Finally, pushing this line of enquiry a bit further, we made another discovery: there are reduced versions of the passage, such as 'Vale. Te amo', which are used extensively by Voltaire, in particular in letters that are part of the social network of old school friends outlined above. This passage is in fact too brief to be identified by our matching algorithms – we identified its usage using *EE*'s simple search interface – and we would be hard-pressed to classify it as a specifically Ciceronian borrowing. Yet we also cannot exclude the possibility – quotations create the expectation of further quotations.

6 Futures

6.1 Digital Readings

Digital readings come in many shapes and sizes. Critics wedded to the traditions of New Criticism and close reading have understandably been cautious about the introduction of digital humanities into literary criticism – a suspicion voiced memorably, and bizarrely, by Stanley Fish, when he writes that digital humanities are opposed to what has always been his aim as a literary critic, 'a desire for pre-eminence, authority and disciplinary power' (Fish, 2012).

No less polemical in its origin, Franco Moretti's coining of the term 'distant reading', used both as a foil against close reading and literary canonicity, posits distance as a new 'condition of knowledge' and way of knowing for literary studies in which 'the text itself disappears'. In this new framework, which has recently become synonymous with quantitative computational analysis and large-scale data visualisations, 'if we want to understand the [literary] system in its entirety', Moretti tells us, 'we must accept losing something' (Moretti, 2013, p. 49). It is hardly a stretch to link these two extremes, identifying Moretti's 'something' to be lost with the very notion of disciplinary authority upheld by Fish and others.

But could this dichotomy of close and distant reading be a false or misleading one? And how might both approaches be assimilated in a critical reading, or better yet, in a critical edition?

There is nothing new about having to confront changes in the way we read – Voltaire's generation also lived through what has been called a reading revolution. In his work on the history of reading in early modern Germany, Rolf Engelsing (1974) showed how a shift in literary production away from theological or devotional works in favour of more worldly literature, including fiction and philosophy, was accompanied from the middle of the eighteenth century by a change from 'intensive' to 'extensive' reading. The creation of the Enlightenment reading public was thus marked by, if not distant, at least broader reading and the emergence of new genres like the novel appropriate to this secular individual imagination. Voltaire's highly cultivated use of literary quotation in his epistolary writing, adjusted according to the gender of his correspondent, is a small but telling example of his sensitivity to readership(s).

Recent studies have emphasised the use of distant reading to describe the larger landscape of literary history (Underwood, 2019), where large datasets can be used to chart changes in punctuation in a literary genre over a period of time, to model the fuzzy distinction between 'high' and 'low' poetry over a century's worth of literary reviews, or to study patterns of emplotment: for Andrew Piper, the essential challenge is to understand the significance of quantity for the study of literature (Piper, 2018). Such literary investigations are fundamentally different from – though they may be complementary to – exercises in close reading.

Rejecting the opposition of close and distant reading, Katherine Bode (2018) argues for a new form of data-rich literary history that incorporates the values and insights of the traditional scholarly edition – and here we wonder how the riches of Besterman's edition might in the future be used to generate further digital investigations. The strength of Bode's argument rests on the notion that literary 'systems' – those that Moretti and Underwood are trying to map and analyse – are in themselves complex bibliographical (and historical) objects and should be treated with the same care and critical acumen as scholarly editions of single works. At the other extreme of this spectrum would be large uncurated and uncorrected collections such as Google Books, the deficiencies of which are masked by the sheer size of its holdings. Bigger, in this case, is not always better.

Other researchers have developed methods that enable various types of interpretative exercises at different ends of the close/distant spectrum, like the set of analytical tools called Voyant, which can be embedded into an essay or blog published online (Rockwell & Sinclair, 2016). This takes a similar approach to what we have attempted here, as Voyant effectively combines the ability to perform close reading at a distance – mapping repeated terms over a combined corpus, for instance – or, seen the other way round, distant reading up close, such as visualising the story arc of one character in one particular text.

As we have attempted to show in the previous sections, digital approaches can, and should, enable both close and distant reading, non-exclusively. Our notion of digital readings in this book is thus one based on a productive telescoping between the fine grain of literary expression and the larger social and cultural systems at play in the eighteenth century. As both a literary monument and a social document, Voltaire's correspondence provides in many ways a perfect test case for new approaches aimed at understanding – and making sense of – today's growing digital archives. Individual letters convey meaning and emotion, humour and philosophical ideas, but they rarely do so in a vacuum. Only at a certain critical distance can we begin to see the topology of the entire correspondence – of the shapes and forms that only become legible once seen from far enough away.

Digital and computational approaches are especially good at generating this kind of algorithmic or programmatic distance, but it is up to those who use and develop these methods to ensure that traditional interpretative strategies are never far from hand. We have based our readings on traces – names, neologisms, quotations – that exist unequivocally in our corpus but that are given new purchase when considered *en masse* and linked to other collections. Other approaches, those that bleed into the worlds of information retrieval, text mining, and machine learning, tend to lead us progressively away from the texts themselves – thus confirming Moretti's intuition that at a distance 'the text itself disappears', making it difficult to enact any sort of close reading, at least in the traditional sense. Yet, as Piper (2015) has claimed, perhaps close and distant reading necessarily coalesce into the same interpretative process for digital humanities work, one in which computational models rather than texts become the primary objects of literary interpretation.

For our part, it was important for us to present digital experiments and methods with relatively low barriers of entry for non-technical readers. While not intended as a 'how-to' guide, our aim was to explore the potential of digital resources to generate new knowledge when brought into conversation with each other. Obviously, we recognise the immense privilege we have benefited from concerning access to collections and technical infrastructure at our respective institutions. Nonetheless, we are confident that the techniques outlined above, which require no proprietary software or deep technical skills, can be effectively applied to any correspondence collection no matter its size or linguistic expression. Methods as straightforward as text encoding and data extraction can lead us to explore questions concerning Voltaire's correspondence in new ways, offering fresh evidence for his relevance over the past two and half centuries. Other, more complex methods such as sequence alignment enable us to unearth new questions that would have been difficult to pose outside of the digital reading environment. In both cases, we remain methodologically anchored to the texts themselves, whether Voltaire's or Manilius', in an effort to move between large-scale distant readings and close reading at scale. These experiments thus demonstrate, we hope, that the gap between distant and close reading is perhaps not all that significant, even today, and that in the not-too-distant future, it may well disappear altogether.

From digitisation to data mining, interpretation to artificial intelligence, the spectrum of digital approaches to text collections such as Voltaire's correspondence is broad and far-reaching. One of the current 'low-hanging fruits' in the digital humanities, for example, is to be found in so-called linked open data (LOD) techniques. A major field of inquiry that encompasses large-scale archival practices, natural language processing, and semantic web technologies (Heath & Bizer, 2011), LOD provides a reference framework in which digital collections, if structured appropriately, can be intelligently linked with other related collections automatically. Clearly, LOD has great potential for digital correspondences; the many data points contained therein – people, places, events, dates, institutions, scientific and literary works, and so on – can be harvested, catalogued, and linked to international authority bases at a much lower cost of intellectual labour than before, when each point had to be identified, annotated, and defined by hand. Our use of the Procope ontology of French correspondents in Section 5 was just a small taste of how open and linked data might enrich correspondences. These efficiencies of scale are important and mean that even small, bespoke projects can insert themselves into the global LOD ecosystem with the right data model. Moreover, semantic linking means that single texts, whether literary or epistolary, can be brought into conversation with other texts from diverse domains – literature, intellectual and literary history, art history, cultural history, music, philosophy, history of science, and others – thus realising a fundamentally interdisciplinary approach that, incidentally, echoes the Enlightenment's own practice of transdisciplinarity.

If we choose to think of each of Voltaire's letters as a node in a network – to borrow the dominant information metaphor of our time – it is a network that stretches out in concentric circles from friends and family to the upper echelons of European nobility. Other connections of all sorts – personal, professional, social, intellectual, political – can be mapped, visualised, and conceptualised through the establishment and exploitation of enriched metadata and relational databases (Edmondson & Edelstein, 2019). But beyond these 'small world' distant readings there lies an even smaller world of lexical and semantic connections, of literary expression and allusion, of critical analyses and judgements that remains to be explored and exploited in interesting ways. As we have seen, digital methods, some old and many new, are well suited for this task of opening up complex collections such as correspondences for analysis on multiple scales, from close to distant and back again. As digitised collections continue to grow, these new reading and research activities will need to grow apace.

One of the earliest entrants in the domain of computer-assisted analysis of texts, stylometry has for the past half century worked to tackle complex literary questions such as stylistic individuation, collaborative writing, and authorship attribution, and all at the scale of single texts (Holmes, 1998; Delcourt, 2002). By and large, stylometric approaches attempt to group texts together by identifying patterns of lexical expression that are often hidden from the human eye; the unremarkable usage of function words, repeated punctuation, and other stylistic tics, all of which rely on the fine-grained analysis of carefully selected and corrected corpora. Use-case scenarios for the stylometric analysis of letters abound: clustering letters by stylistic expression and particular correspondents; analysing the style of public versus private letters; modelling the 'epistolarity' of fictional letters compared to real letters; suggesting authorship for anonymous or apocryphal letters, and so on. Though decidedly small-scale in their object of analysis, stylometric approaches can be highly complex in their computational elaboration.

Equally complex in their computational nature, but focussed on categorically larger-scale text collections, recent developments in recursive neural networks and word embeddings could also be of interest for the analysis of large correspondences such as Voltaire's. Popularised by Google's 'word2vec' word-embedding model,[30] vector space approaches to humanities text collections have recently become more prevalent in the wider digital humanities world (Schmidt, 2015), addressing diverse topics such as diachronic semantic shifts in historical texts and, if one can believe it, William Empson's notion of ambiguity (Hamilton et al., 2016; Gavin, 2018). For Voltaire, whose long career was witness to a great many shifts in conceptual and linguistic acceptations, one could imagine mapping his 'vector semantics' using a word-embedding model pre-trained on eighteenth-century French texts. This would allow us to plot concepts (tolerance, superstition, materialism, Newtonianism, religion, etc.) in high-dimensional 'vector space' and track their relative shifts over the course of his long writing career. We could equally explore how concepts evolve, are exchanged, and eventually die out as literary tastes or social situations change. Here, Voltaire's place at the very heart of the French Enlightenment and the larger European Republic of Letters makes his correspondence an invaluable corpus for such large-scale analysis and exploration.

6.2 An Experiment in Topic Modelling

As a nod to the possible directions some of these future research avenues might take, we offer in closing one final digital experiment using a machine-learning approach that has lately taken root in the digital humanities: the suite of unsupervised learning algorithms commonly known as 'topic modelling' (Blei, 2012). Topic models are built on the notion that a single text, or document, in a given corpus is comprised of one or more 'topics' – that is, clusters of closely related words that tend to co-occur over the entire corpus. These topics can be used as a form of exploratory data analysis on large heterogeneous collections that otherwise lack indices or other organising structures; topic models are often an efficient means to summarise, visualise, explore, and theorise about texts at scale, without reading them in any traditional sense. Clearly, this sort of automatic indexing holds great potential for correspondence collections, which often have little or no organisational principles other than chronology. To test the promise and peril of this sort of maximally distant

---

[30] https://code.google.com/archive/p/word2vec/.

Figure 6.1 Topic model (40 topics) of 15,414 letters by Voltaire

approach, we built a topic model of Voltaire's letters, which we briefly explore below.[31]

After removing function words (small, high-frequency terms), and normalising for case and accents, we trained our model on lemmatised forms of single words and bi-grams (e.g., words that co-occur, such as 'pere famille' for 'père de famille') in order to generate an arbitrary number of topics chosen at the pre-processing state.[32] The forty topics constructed by the algorithm immediately provided us with unexpected points of entry into Voltaire's more than 15,000 letters (see Fig. 6.1).

---

[31] We are most grateful to Clovis Gladstone of the ARTFL project at the University of Chicago, who prepared this experiment.

[32] For more on the algorithm and browser used to build our model, see the ARTFL Research blog post: https://artfl.blogspot.com/2020/01/modeling-revolutionary-discourse.html.

Of course, some of the topics are reassuringly predictable: Topic 0 (idea, nature, matter, reason, body, force, truth, thing, light, mind) is a cluster of philosophical terms that reminds us of the centrality of Enlightenment philosophy in many of these letters. Topic 4 (philosopher, philosophy, book, reason, Jean, author, article, priest, tolerance, honest) provides a similar cluster around the related question of religious 'toleration' – again, this is a predictable cluster of thoughts, even if the presence of the proper name 'Jean' might require further investigation.

Voltaire's philosophy is inseparable from campaigning in the high-profile Calas and Sirven affairs, hence Topic 39 (Sirven, judge, Calas, Toulouse, brochure, lawyer, innocence, family, fanaticism, parliament, Toulouse). From here it is not far to Topic 7 around the idea of religion: 'God, thanks, thanks to God, saint, Jesuit, Pope, priest, devil, beautiful, poor'. Books, writing, literature are clearly important and are reflected in several topics (5, 19, 20, 29, and 36), while theatre, a life-long passion for Voltaire, is central to Topics 3, 28, 37, and 38.

Other topics strike us as somewhat random and do not immediately offer any particular insight, for example Topic 33: 'house, country, garden, master, servant, step, day, town, horse, palace'. Others identify a theme that we recognise from the letters, though perhaps we had not appreciated its full importance. Voltaire is a hypochondriac, and Topic 27 reminds us of this: 'Health, Colmar, child, water, niece, all, doctor, Plombières, journey, illness'; his valetudinarian concerns with ageing and death similarly make up Topic 15. Voltaire's correspondence requires a lot of managing, and we can easily overlook this constant preoccupation in the letters, hence the interest of Topic 26: 'Packet, post, address, large, large packet, path, mail, envelope, copy, reply'. Two of the topics (6 and 13) indeed seem to derive specifically from the formulations typically found in the subscription (signing off) of the letter.

It would, of course, be possible to conduct further topic modelling with restricted parts of the corpus: one could search the letters omitting the subscription, for example; or one could model the topics for different decades and try to ascertain if certain themes become less or more prominent in time: Topic 23 clusters references to Geneva, the lake, and the mountains, so there would be no surprise if this topic figured particularly strongly in the letters written after 1755, when Voltaire was living in or near Geneva.

For simplicity, it is tempting to try to reduce each topic to a single theme, but it is worth noting how often contraries co-exist. Thus, Topic 15 includes, alongside 'pain', 'age' and 'death', 'life', 'consolation', and 'happiness'; Topic 21 juxtaposes the key term 'toleration' with 'Jesuit' and 'Pompignan', one of Voltaire's most famous enemies: it is out of oppositions such as these that Voltaire's characteristic thinking is forged.

Above all, these topics can remind us of themes that we risk underestimating or overlooking. Voltaire is, of course, a philosopher, but at the same time he is a businessman who is independently wealthy, and many of these letters have nothing to do with the Enlightenment and everything to do with business. Witness Topic 10: 'money, pound, note, sum, month, account, exchange, rent, letter of change, year'. Topic 1 also is remarkable: 'war, France, peace, army, English, prince, England, troops, Europe, battle'. The Enlightenment is played out against a backdrop of sometimes fierce conflict, and the Seven Years' War (which provides the context of *Candide*) was especially difficult for Voltaire, who had earlier made his name as an Anglophile; this topic reminds us starkly of one of Voltaire's significant underlying worries. In the future we aim to make a model of Voltaire's topics available online as part of the Voltaire Lab, with a new interface (see Fig. 6.2) to allow readers additional inroads into the correspondence and its contents.[33]

6.3 Final Thoughts

The methods described in this Element and here applied to Voltaire's correspondence are equally applicable to other similar corpora and datasets. As life-writing becomes an increasingly fruitful domain of enquiry, for example, the social nature of texts such as letters and autobiographical writings can only be explored in greater depth by the methods and techniques described above. Voltaire's letters are short works of considerable literary complexity, and they relate to each other to form groups and networks in intricate and unexpected ways: only the use of digital methods can help to approach this corpus from the perspective of both close and distant reading. Such methods aid us in constructing the correspondence as an object of study and also, as in the case of topic modelling, in de-constructing it. In all cases, these new forms of reading – both distant and close – can provide invaluable insights into what are often intractable collections of texts.

European writers and readers of Voltaire's generation felt deep unease about the sheer proliferation of printed books – an early example of the fear of distant reading. In his utopian novel *L'An 2440*, Louis-Sébastien Mercier dreams that scholars have distilled the contents of a thousand folio volumes in the Royal Library into one tiny duodecimo book (Mercier, 1771, chap. 30). But in his *Questions sur l'Encyclopédie*, published the year before, in 1770, Voltaire revels in the fathomless collections of the Royal Library in Paris, which make it possible for readers to focus on the specific works that interest them. The

---

[33] See TopoLogic: https://github.com/ARTFL-Project/TopoLogic.

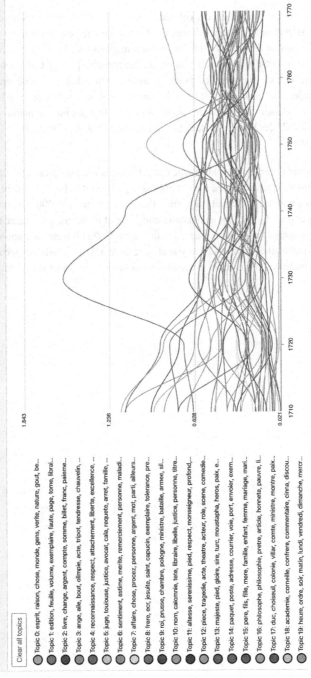

Figure 6.2 Topic model exploration of Voltaire's letters using TopoLogic

digital experiments outlined in this essay have been designed precisely as Voltaire describes, to help us focus on small parts of large wholes:

> Une grande bibliothèque a cela de bon, qu'elle effraie celui qui la regarde. Deux cent mille volumes découragent un homme tenté d'imprimer. […] Il est vrai que dans cette immense collection de livres, il y en a environ cent quatre-vingt-dix-neuf mille qu'on ne lira jamais. […] Cette multitude étonnante de livres ne doit point épouvanter. On a déjà remarqué que Paris contient environ sept cent mille hommes, qu'on ne peut vivre avec tous, et qu'on choisit trois ou quatre amis. Ainsi il ne faut pas plus se plaindre de la multitude des livres, que de celle des citoyens. (Voltaire, 1968–2021, vol. 39, p. 360)

A great library has the advantage that it frightens whoever looks at it. 200,000 volumes can discourage a man tempted to go into print. […] It is true that in this immense collection of books, there are around 199,000 that one will never read. […] This astonishing multitude of books must not scare us. We have already noted that Paris contains about 700,000 men, that you cannot live with all of them, and that you choose three or four friends. So one should no more complain about the multitude of books than about the multitude of citizens.

Abbreviations

ARTFL	*Project for American and French Research on the Treasury of the French Language*
D	Voltaire (1968–2021), vol. 85–135, *Correspondence and related documents*
EE	*Electronic Enlightenment*
PHI	*Packard Humanities Institute – Classical Latin Texts*
TLF	*Trésor de la langue française*
TLFi	*Trésor de la langue française informatisé*

References

Allen, T., Morrissey, R., & Roe, G. (2011). Re-imagining French lexicography: the Dictionnaire vivant de la langue française. *Dictionaries: Journal of the Dictionary Society of North America*, 32, 129–43.

Beauzée, N. (1765). Néologique, Néologue. In D. Diderot and J. D'Alembert, eds., *Encyclopédie, ou dictionnaire raisonné des sciences, des arts et des métiers*, vol. XI. Paris: Libraires associés.

Bednarz, J. P. (2018). Shakespeare and the early modern culture of quotation. In J. Maxwell and K. Rumbold, eds., *Shakespeare and Quotation*. Cambridge: Cambridge University Press, 1–45.

Bessire, F. (1999). *La Bible dans la correspondence de Voltaire*. Oxford: Voltaire Foundation.

Blei, D. (2012). Topic Modeling and Digital Humanities. *Journal of Digital Humanities* 2(1). http://journalofdigitalhumanities.org/2–1/topic-modeling-and-digital-humanities-by-david-m-blei/

Bode, K. (2018). *A World of Fiction: Digital Collections and the Future of Literary History*. Ann Arbor: University of Michigan Press.

Bolton, J., & Grusin, R. (2000). *Remediation: Understanding New Media*. Cambridge: Massachusetts Institute of Technology Press.

Brockliss, L. (2002). *Calvet's Web: Enlightenment and the Republic of Letters in Eighteenth-Century France*. Oxford: Oxford University Press.

Brunot, F. (1932). *La Langue post-classique. Vol. VI of Histoire de la langue française des origines à 1900*. Paris: A. Colin.

Calvez, D. (1989). *Le Langage proverbial de Voltaire dans sa correspondance (1704–1769)*, Berne: Peter Lang.

Clemit, P. (2019). The signal of regard: William Godwin's correspondence networks. *European Romantic Review*, 30(4), 353–66.

Comsa, M., Conroy, M., Edelstein, D., Edmondson, C., & Willan, C. (2016). The French Enlightenment network. *Journal of Modern History*, 88, 495–534.

Cotoni, M.-H. (1995). Le rire, la plainte et le cri dans les dernières années de la *Correspondance* de Voltaire. In C. Biondi, et al., eds., *La Quête du bonheur et l'expression de la douleur dans la littérature et la pensée françaises: Mélanges offerts à Corrado Rosso*. Geneva: Droz, pp. 46–75.

Cronk, N. (2007). Voltaire autoplagiaire. In O. Ferret, G. Goggi, & C. Volpilhac-Auger, eds., *Copier/coller. Écriture et réécriture chez Voltaire*. Pisa: PLUS, pp. 9–28.

Cronk, N. (2016a). La correspondance entre Voltaire et le duc d'Uzès: compléments à l'édition Besterman (D4585-R1, D6248-R1, D7134a). *Dix-huitième siècle*, 48, 607–31.

Cronk, N. (2016b). Voltaire and the chevalier de Jaucourt: the lessons of an epistolary corpus. *Revue Voltaire*, 16, 215–27.

Cronk, N. (2019). Voltaire's correspondence network: questions of exploration and interpretation. In C. Edmondson & D. Edelstein, eds., *Networks of Enlightenment: digital approaches to the Republic of Letters. Oxford University Studies in the Enlightenment*. Liverpool: Liverpool University Press, pp. 23–46.

Cronk, N. (2021). Electronic Enlightenment: recreating the Republic of Letters. In S. Burrows & G. Roe, eds., *Digitizing Enlightenment: digital humanities and the transformation of eighteenth-century studies. Oxford University Studies in the Enlightenment*. Liverpool: Liverpool University Press, pp. 55–72.

Cronk, N., & McNamee, R. (2005). Le projet *Electronic Enlightenment* de la Voltaire Foundation. *Cahiers de l'AIEF (CAIEF)*, 57, 303–11.

Dainville, F. (1978). *L'Education des jésuites (XVIe-XVIIIe siècles)*. Paris: Minuit.

Dawson, D. (1994). *Voltaire's Correspondence: An Epistolary Novel*. New York: Peter Lang.

Delattre, A. (1952). *Répertoire chronologique des lettres de Voltaire non recueillies dans les éditions de sa correspondance générale*. Chapel Hill: University of North Carolina Press.

Delcourt, C. (2002). Stylometry. *Revue belge de philologie et d'histoire*, 80(3), 979–1002.

Delon, M. (1984). 'Homo sum … ' Un vers de Térence comme devise des Lumières. *Dix-huitième siècle*, 16, 279–96.

Diderot, D. (1755). Encyclopédie. In D. Diderot & J. D'Alembert, eds., *Encyclopédie, ou dictionnaire raisonnés des sciences, des arts et des métiers*, vol. 5. Paris: Libraires associés.

Diepeveen, L. (1993). *Changing Voices: The Modern Quoting Poem*. Ann Arbor: University of Michigan Press.

Edelstein, D. (2008). Humanism, l'esprit philosophique, and the Encyclopédie. *Republics of Letters* 1(1). http://rofl.stanford.edu/node/27

Edelstein, D. (2016). Intellectual history and digital humanities. *Modern Intellectual History*, 13, 237–46.

Edelstein, D. (2019). Voltaire's European correspondents: an Enlightenment network? In L. Andriès & M. A. Bernier, eds., *L'Avenir des Lumières: The Future of Enlightenment*. Paris: Hermann.

Edelstein, D. (2021). Mapping the Republic of Letters: history of a digital humanities project. In S. Burrows & G. Roe, eds., *Digitizing Enlightenment: digital humanities and the transformation of eighteenth-century studies. Oxford University Studies in the Enlightenment.* Liverpool: Liverpool University Press, pp. 73–88.

Edelstein, D., & Kassabova, B. (2018). How England fell off the map of Voltaire's Enlightenment. *Modern Intellectual History*, 1–25. doi:https://doi.org/10.1017/S147924431800015X

Edelstein, D., Morrissey, R., & Roe, G. (2013). To quote or not to quote: citation strategies in the Encyclopédie. *Journal of the History of Ideas*, 74(2), 213–36.

Edmondson, C., & Edelstein, D., eds. (2019). *Networks of Enlightenment: Digital Approaches to the Republic of Letters. Oxford University Studies in the Enlightenment.* Liverpool: Liverpool University Press.

Engelsing, R. (1974). *Der Bürger als Leser: Lesergeschichte in Deutschland 1500–1800.* Stuttgart: Metzler.

Falk, I., Bernhard, D., & Gérard, C. (2014). From non word to new word: automatically identifying neologisms in French newspapers. *Proceedings of the Ninth International Conference on Language Resources and Evaluation (LREC).*

Fish, S. (2012). The digital humanities and the transcending of mortality. *The New York Times*, 9 January 2012.

Fumaroli, M. (2003). L'anti-Emile: Voltaire et ses éducateurs jésuites. *Revue Voltaire*, 3, 217–32.

Gavin, M. (2018). Vector semantics, William Empson, and the study of ambiguity. *Critical Inquiry*, 44, 641–73.

Gibert, P. (2010). *L'Invention critique de la Bible, XVe–XVIIIe siècle.* Paris: Gallimard-NRF.

Goyet, F. (1996). *Le Sublime du 'lieu commun'. L'Invention rhétorique dans l'Antiquité et à la Renaissance.* Paris: Honoré Champion.

Hamilton, W., Leskovec, J., & Jarafsky, D. (2016). Diachronic word embeddings reveal statistical laws of semantic change. *Proceedings of the 54th Annual Meeting of the Association for Computational Linguistics*, 1489–501.

Heath, T., & Bizer, C. (2011). *Linked Data: Evolving the Web into a Global Data Space.* San Rafael: Morgan & Claypool.

Holmes, D. (1998). The evolution of stylometry in humanities scholarship. *Literary and Linguistic Computing*, 13(3), 111–17.

Hotson, H., & Wallnig, T., eds. (2019). *Reassembling the Republic of Letters in the Digital Age: Standards, Systems, Scholarship.* Göttingen: Göttingen University Press.

Lilti, A. (2014). *Figures publiques: l'invention de la célébrité 1750–1850.* Paris: Fayard.

McGann, J. (1991). *The Textual Condition.* Princeton: Princeton University Press.

McGann, J. (2006). From text to work: digital tools and the emergence of the social text. *Text,* 16, 49–62.

McKenzie, D. (1999). *Bibliography and the Sociology of Texts.* Cambridge: Cambridge University Press.

Mercier, L.-S. (1771). *L'An 2440.* Amsterdam: E. Van Harrevelt.

Mercier, L.-S. (2009). *Néologie.* Paris: Bellin.

Mervaud, C. (2009). Voltaire's correspondence. In N. Cronk, ed., *The Cambridge Companion to Voltaire.* Cambridge: Cambridge University Press, 153–65.

Mervaud, M. (2011). Voltaire lexicographe: note sur la néologie, les créations verbales et les mots rares de Voltaire, principalement dans les Questions sur l'Encyclopédie. *Revue Voltaire,* 11, 341–65.

Moncrif, F.-A. (1751). Qu'on ne peut ni ne doit fixer une langue vivante. In *Œuvres,* vol. 2. Paris: Lecteur de la Reine.

Moretti, F. (2000). Conjectures on world literature. *New Left Review,* 1, 54–68.

Moretti, F. (2013). *Distant Reading.* London: Verso.

Norman, L. (2011). *The Shock of the Ancient: Literature and History in Early Modern France.* Chicago: University of Chicago Press.

Olsen, M., Horton, R., & Roe, G. (2011). Something borrowed: sequence alignment and the identification of similar passages in large text collections. *Digital Studies / le Champ Numérique,* 2(1). http://doi.org/10.16995/dscn.258

Pascal, B. (1992). *Œuvres complètes,* vol. 3, ed. J. Mesnard. Paris: Desclée de Brouwer.

Pink, G. (2018). *Voltaire à l'ouvrage.* Paris, CNRS Éditions.

Piper, A. (2015). Novel devotions: conversional reading, computational modeling, and the modern novel. *New Literary History,* 46(1), 63–98.

Piper, A. (2018). *Enumerations: Data and Literary Study.* Chicago: University of Chicago Press.

Rockwell, G., and Sinclair, S. (2016). *Hermeneutica: Computer-Assisted Interpretation in the Humanities.* Cambridge: Massachusetts Institute of Technology Press.

Roe, G. (2012). Intertextuality and influence in the age of Enlightenment: sequence alignment applications for humanities research. *Digital Humanities 2012,* 345–7.

Roe, G. (2018). A sheep in Wolff's clothing: Émilie Du Châtelet and the *Encyclopédie*. *Eighteenth-Century Studies*, 51(2), 179–96.

Schmidt, B. (2015). Vector space models for the digital humanities. [blog post], 25 October: http://bookworm.benschmidt.org/posts/2015-10-25-Word-Embeddings.html.

Seguin, J-P. (1972). *La Langue française au XVIIIe siècle*. Paris: Bordas.

Thomas, K. (1990). Yours. In C. Ricks & L. Michaels, eds., *The State of the Language: 1990s Edition*. London: Faber and Faber, pp. 451–6.

Underwood, T. (2017). A genealogy of distant reading. *Digital Humanities Quarterly*, 11(2).

Underwood, T. (2019). *Distant Horizons: Digital Evidence and Literary Change*. Chicago: University of Chicago Press.

Voltaire. (1784–9). *Œuvres complètes de Voltaire,* 70 vols. Kehl: Société littéraire-typographique.

Voltaire. (1829–34). *Œuvres de Voltaire*, 72 vols. Paris: Lefèvre.

Voltaire. (1968–2021). *Œuvres complètes de Voltaire*, 203 vols. Oxford: Voltaire Foundation.

Voltaire. (2017). *Lettres choisies*. Paris: Gallimard.

Acknowledgements

We are immensely grateful to our series editors, Rebecca Bullard and Eve Tavor Bannet, for their advice and encouragement; to Andrew Kahn and Gillian Pink, who were our first readers; and to the two anonymous readers who made such helpful suggestions. We are also grateful to the John Fell Fund (University of Oxford) for its generous support.

Cambridge Elements ≡

Eighteenth-Century Connections

Series Editors

Eve Tavor Bannet,
University of Oklahoma
Eve Tavor Bannet is George Lynn Cross Professor Emeritus, University of Oklahoma and Editor of *Studies in Eighteenth-Century Culture.* Her monographs include *Empire of Letters: Letter Manuals and Transatlantic Correspondence 1688–1820* (Cambridge, 2005), *Transatlantic Stories and the History of Reading, 1720–1820* (Cambridge, 2011), and *Eighteenth-Century Manners of Reading: Print Culture and Popular Instruction in the Anglophone Atlantic World* (Cambridge, 2017). She is editor of *British and American Letter Manuals 1680–1810* (Pickering & Chatto, 2008), *Emma Corbett* (Broadview, 2011) and with Susan Manning, *Transatlantic Literary Studies* (Cambridge, 2012).

Rebecca Bullard,
University of Reading
Rebecca Bullard is Associate Professor of English Literature at the University of Reading. She is the author of *The Politics of Disclosure: Secret History Narratives, 1674–1725* (Pickering & Chatto, 2009), co-editor of *The Plays and Poems of Nicholas Rowe, volume 1* (Routledge, 2017) and co-editor of *The Secret History in Literature, 1660–1820* (Cambridge, 2017).

Advisory Board

Linda Bree, Independent
Claire Connolly, University College Cork
Gillian Dow, University of Southampton
James Harris, University of St Andrews
Thomas Keymer, University of Toronto
Jon Mee, University of York
Carla Mulford, Penn State University
Nicola Parsons, University of Sydney
Manushag Powell, Purdue University
Robbie Richardson, University of Kent
Shef Rogers, University of Otago
Eleanor Shevlin, West Chester University
David Taylor, Oxford University
Chloe Wigston Smith, University of York
Roxann Wheeler, Ohio State University
Eugenia Zuroski, MacMaster University

About the Series
Exploring connections between verbal and visual texts and the people, networks, cultures and places that engendered and enjoyed them during the long Eighteenth Century, this innovative series also examines the period's uses of oral, written and visual media, and experiments with the digital platform to facilitate communication of original scholarship with both colleagues and students.

Cambridge Elements $\equiv$

Eighteenth-Century Connections

Elements in the Series

Voltaire's Correspondence: Digital Readings
Nicholas Cronk and Glenn Roe

A full series listing is available at: www.cambridge.org/core/what-we-publish/
elements/eighteenth-century-connections

Printed in the United States
By Bookmasters